Mary, Martha, and Me

Mary, Martha, and Me

Seeking *the* One Thing *That Is* Needful

CAMILLE FRONK OLSON

DESERET
BOOK

SALT LAKE CITY, UTAH

The following images are used by permission from their respective copyright holders.

Page 6: *Jesus with Mary and Martha,* by Del Parson. Copyright Intellectual Reserve, Inc. All rights reserved.

Page 87: *Martha, Martha,* by Elspeth Young. Copyright 2005 Elspeth Young. All rights reserved.

Page 121: *Jesus at the Home of Mary and Martha,* by Minerva Teichert. Courtesy of Brigham Young University Museum of Art. All rights reserved.

Library of Congress Cataloging-in-Publication Data

Olson, Camille Fronk.
  Mary, Martha, and me / Camille Fronk Olson.
      p.   cm.
  Includes bibliographical references and index.
  ISBN-10 1-59038-547-0 (hardbound : alk. paper)
  ISBN-13 978-1-59038-547-0 (hardbound : alk. paper)
    1. Mormon women—Religious life.   2. Mary, of Bethany, Saint.
  3. Martha, Saint.   4. Bible. N.T. Luke X, 38-42—Criticism, interpre-
  tation, etc.   I. Title.
  BX8641.O57 2006
  248.4'89332—dc22   2005031751

Printed in the United States of America
R.R. Donnelley and Sons, Crawfordsville, IN

10   9   8   7   6   5   4   3

For Grandma

Luke 10:38–42

Now it came to pass, as they went,

that he entered into a certain village:

and a certain woman named Martha

received him into her house.

And she had a sister called Mary,

which also sat at Jesus' feet,

and heard his word.

But Martha was cumbered about much serving,

and came to him, and said,

Lord, dost thou not care

that my sister hath left me to serve alone?

bid her therefore that she help me.

And Jesus answered and said unto her,

Martha, Martha, thou art careful

and troubled about many things:

But one thing is needful:

and Mary hath chosen that good part,

which shall not be taken away from her.

Contents

CHAPTER ONE

Mixed Messages

Visiting her home in New Testament Bethany, Jesus counseled the multitasking Martha, "One thing is needful" (Luke 10:42). Amid daily demands, high-speed agendas, and information overload that characterize our everyday lives, the Lord's reminder seems overly simple. Emotions that rotate among defeat, anxiety, guilt, and arrogance become all too familiar companions in our attempts to be good disciples of Christ. Where is the balance? Where is the peace? How can "one thing" be the answer?

Through unexpected turns in life, I have often asked these questions. Just as often, I have sensed seemingly mixed messages that have added confusion. How can you be "anxiously engaged in a good cause, and do many things of [your] own free will" (D&C 58:27) and also "be still and know that [He is]

1

God"? (D&C 101:16). How do you apply the counsel "reduce and simplify" when Church commitments compete with home responsibilities most nights of the week? How do you choose "less" when "more" is so easily acquired and publicly applauded?

In a world that thrives on comparison and competition, our souls yearn for one needful thing to bring the weightier matters into focus and provide clear direction for our hectic schedules today and all our demanding tomorrows.

I have found insight, divine direction, and reassurance through scriptural examples and teachings. In the case of Christ's instruction to Martha, it was my grandmother Harris who sparked the insights. Grandma was already an important role model in my youth, but her influence became most poignant after her death more than twenty years ago. Reflections on our conversations shortly before she died have illuminated the timeliness of biblical passages involving Mary and Martha.

Grandma was a hard worker. She rose long before the sun and attacked scores of domestic projects until late into the night. She was a remarkable seamstress, gardener, quilter, laundress, and cook. Grandma was devoted to the Relief Society and took pride in her ability to whip up a casserole, dinner rolls, or pie whenever compassionate service was needed for another family in the ward. She literally wore out her life in the service of others. In so many ways, she seemed to epitomize what God wants His daughters to become.

In her exemplary position, Grandma was also hard to help. Her standards surpassed almost everyone's abilities, especially mine. I knew this because my mother compared her own pies and quilts and vigor in sweeping the floor with Grandma's and always admitted inferiority. I, in turn, compared my abilities with my mother's, which was no comparison at all. It became all too apparent all too soon that we were losing the substance of true womanhood with each passing generation.

All these expectations followed me as I was welcomed into Relief Society at age eighteen. This was God's organization to transform girls into women of purpose, righteousness, and beauty. With the motto "Charity Never Faileth," I had high expectations for an education that would finally help me achieve my grandmother's domestic stature.

Relief Society teachers frequently referred to women in scripture to inspire and inform our perspectives of who we can become. Particularly popular in my young adult Relief Society was the virtuous woman of Proverbs 31, whose value far exceeded rubies:

> *Who can find a virtuous woman? for her price is far above rubies.*

The heart of her husband doth safely trust in her, so that he shall have no need of spoil.

She will do him good and not evil all the days of her life.

She seeketh wool, and flax, and worketh willingly with her hands.

She is like the merchants' ships; she bringeth her food from afar.

She riseth also while it is yet night, and giveth meat to her household, and a portion to her maidens.

She considereth a field, and buyeth it: with the fruit of her hands she planteth a vineyard.

She girdeth her loins with strength, and strengtheneth her arms.

She perceiveth that her merchandise is good: her candle goeth not out by night.

She layeth her hands to the spindle, and her hands hold the distaff.

She stretcheth out her hand to the poor; yea, she reacheth forth her hands to the needy.

She is not afraid of the snow for her household: for all her household are clothed with scarlet.

She maketh herself coverings of tapestry; her clothing is silk and purple.

Her husband is known in the gates, when he sitteth among the elders of the land.

She maketh fine linen, and selleth it; and delivereth girdles unto the merchant.

Strength and honour are her clothing; and she shall rejoice in time to come.

She openeth her mouth with wisdom; and in her
tongue is the law of kindness.
　　She looketh well to the ways of her household, and
eateth not the bread of idleness.
　　Her children arise up, and call her blessed; her hus-
band also, and he praiseth her.
　　Many daughters have done virtuously, but thou
excellest them all.
　　Favour is deceitful, and beauty is vain: but a
woman that feareth the Lord, she shall be praised.
　　Give her of the fruit of her hands; and let her own
works praise her in the gates. (Vv. 10–31)

We college-age women interpreted this passage of scripture to mean that the ideal woman never lets anything spoil
(v. 11); sews and creates with fabric (v. 13); never sleeps late
but begins her work before sunrise (v. 15); plants a garden and
reaps the harvest (v. 16); works through most of the night
(v. 18); cares for the poor and the needy (v. 20); dresses beautifully (v. 22); and speaks with a gentle, sweet voice (v. 26).
That was my grandmother. She was the personification of
Proverbs 31.

Later, as I attended Relief Society with women of all ages
and circumstances, I noticed a different story emerge as the
favorite scriptural model of womanhood—the example of the
New Testament sisters Mary and Martha. The Luke 10
account has been represented at church in a variety of ways: a

Jesus with Mary and Martha, by Del Parson

painting of the two sisters is typical décor in Relief Society classrooms; the class manual has included illustrations of Mary and Martha; and an application of the account often comes up in lessons. The best-known painting depicts Martha standing, mixing something in a bowl, as she listens to the Lord's teachings while Mary sits enthralled at Jesus' feet.

Because the story was well known and time was always short in Relief Society, we rarely consulted the account in the scriptures but rather paraphrased key points. Particularly vulnerable to paraphrasing was the Lord's counsel to Martha, the sister "cumbered about much serving" (Luke 10:40). We usually misquoted Jesus as saying, "One thing is needful; Mary chose *the better* part." So I concluded that Jesus was saying that studying truth, learning facts, and sitting still while pondering were "the better part" and therefore the "one thing" necessary. I was surprised to discover, years later, that the comparative word *better* doesn't appear in this scriptural account. The King James Bible reads, "One thing is needful: and Mary hath chosen *that good* part" (Luke 10:42; emphasis added). Acknowledging the absence of comparison in the Lord's response inspired numerous scriptural insights—but not for many years.

My false perception that Christ was comparing Martha's service with Mary's service highlighted the ever-increasing disconnect in my efforts to understand what God wanted in me as a disciple. Was I to be like Mary with a singular focus on gospel study or the Proverbs 31 woman who sounds a lot like Martha? Counsel in formal settings directed me to Mary, but all the activities and examples around me communicated that Martha is our ideal of Christian womanhood.

Furthermore, Grandma was not a Mary. I could never remember seeing Grandma read a book or hearing her talk about things she learned from books, least of all the scriptures. She married young and began her family immediately without another thought of formal study. Once I started college, she was interested in how often I dated, not what I was learning in school or from the gospel. She was concerned that I not neglect the boys along the way and get so smart that no man would want to marry me. No, Grandma was not a Mary.

Until shortly before she died, that is. Then something happened to change Grandma's focus from marriage and homemaking as every girl's primary goal to gaining an understanding of Jesus Christ and His plan for her.

I don't know when it occurred, but I noticed the change during my visits soon after I was hired to teach seminary to LDS high school students. By this time, Grandma's eyesight had been dramatically diminished by macular degeneration. Whenever I visited, she brought out the same book and asked me to read to her. The book was marked about a quarter of the way through, indicating she had started it before her eyesight changed or someone else had been reading it to her.

I never registered the title of the book. It was a fictitious story set in modern times that awkwardly drew on scriptural teachings to resolve conflicts. Not at all captivated by the book, I concluded it was a rather weak way to teach powerful principles. But Grandma wanted to hear it, and I was happy I could do something to help her.

We rarely made it through many pages before Grandma stopped me and asked a doctrinal question sparked by something in the book. Because she asked very basic questions that were in my area of confidence, I was thrilled to give my explanation. At first I wondered if she orchestrated these exchanges in an attempt to show she recognized a talent in me, but I quickly rejected that idea when the ensuing discussion was meaningful and obviously important to her. In subsequent visits, she needed to hear me read only a paragraph or two from her book to launch into her gospel inquiry. Questions seemed to cascade from her as though they had been bottled up for ages. All her concerns seemed to relate to the plan of salvation. Receiving a quick answer was clearly not enough; she wanted to understand.

Grandma died before we made it halfway through the

book. She slipped away the morning after one of our doctrinal discussions. For some time after her death, I wondered what had fascinated her about that book. Though I will never know for sure, I believe it wasn't the book itself that interested her but rather its random references to an aspect of the plan of salvation.

I wondered why she chose to wade through a tiresome narrative, irrelevant to her personal quest, instead of going directly to scripture or a doctrinal book that overtly dealt with these truths. Had she ever pondered the scriptures to receive personal direction and eternal perspective? Perhaps "made-up stories" represented her principal mode for learning and teaching the gospel. Somehow, in all her church attendance, compassionate service, and homemaking, she seemed to have missed the doctrine. With her focus on doing, she naturally found the answer for every human need through a hot meal, clean water, or a needle and thread.

And then, with a clearer view of her mortality, Grandma began to thirst for the doctrine. She yearned for the peace and personal hope that come only from God. Because she lost her eyesight and couldn't *do* all the things anymore that she was used to doing, she was left to her thoughts in a way she probably never had allowed before. With time to finally ponder, she realized important questions pertaining to God and her life after death. What will happen to me? How do I know if I have done what God wants me to do? Does He really love and accept me and my offering? Without recognizing acceptance and comfort communicated by the Spirit, she feared she hadn't done enough. Here was a woman who had spent her life serving others, working hard every day, never shirking her duty toward her family, her neighbors, her Church—and she feared it wasn't enough.

Many times I have wished to return to those afternoons with Grandma, better understanding what she yearned to understand. Why didn't I pull out the scriptures and let the voice of the Lord and His prophets answer her? Truths about each of us and our relationship with God are most meaningful *and believable* when communicated to our spirits by the Lord's Spirit. Furthermore, reading and pondering the scriptural text is a sure invitation to the Spirit to teach an honest seeker of truth.

And I would tell Grandma what a blessing her life has been to me. Her example of finding joy in service has inspired, strengthened, and directed me through uncertain times in my life. Surely the Lord accepted her service and sacrifice—and wanted to tell her so. But she needed to hear it from Him, and that meant she needed to know Him and ask Him with faith. No one could do that for her.

Specifically, I would have read to her the stories of Mary and Martha, highlighting the Lord's teachings to them. I would tell her that the scriptures do not read that the Lord thought Mary's actions are "better" than Martha's service to Him. But the scriptures do read, "One thing is needful." Coming to Him, trusting Him as the Author and Finisher of our faith, and accepting His enabling power as the source of all our successes make our service pure and selfless. Both sisters learned to embrace those truths, and each gave acceptable service to the Lord as a result.

Jesus Christ is the one needful thing. What does that mean amid chaotic daily agendas and anxious uncertainty for the future? The world urges us to strictly follow step-by-step formulas to achieve success. In striking contrast, the Savior taught, "Come unto me" (Matthew 11:28). In my life of never-ending responsibilities, I do not need another checklist (derived from scripture or anywhere else) to define the Lord's role for me. I need Him. I do not need competition that scrutinizes my productivity versus another's efforts to make me a valuable employee; I need His strength, His wisdom, His grace to perform work that will make a difference.

An analysis of the outcomes, resultant attitudes, or "fruit" of the checklist approach versus trusting in the Savior's grace discloses significant differences. The Apostle Paul taught that the fruit "of the flesh" includes a sense of inferiority, pride, impatience, dissatisfaction, jealousy, and contention (see Galatians 5:19–21). The focus of that approach is on *our contribution* and not on the Savior's enabling power, making comparison with another's service hard to avoid. The "fruit of the Spirit," on the other hand, is "love, joy, peace, longsuffering, gentleness, goodness, faith, meekness, [and] temperance" (Galatians 5:22–23). When we remember Him, we take the focus off ourselves and, turning outward, allow the healing power of Christ to take the lead.

This book is for all of us who have confused "Mary's part" or "Martha's part" as the one needful thing. It is for all of us who fear we can never know enough or do enough to be within the grasp of our just and merciful Redeemer. It is an invitation to realign our focus away from the search for a perfect formula toward finding Christ and internalizing His truths. The message of Mary and Martha is not a generic, black-and-white answer to align me with one or the other of them. On the contrary, they give me confidence to ask God directly what He wants me—specifically me—to do.

In a reinforcing way, through this scriptural journey with Mary and Martha, this book is for those who have previously missed the sweetness of communion with the Lord directly through His scriptures. It includes the invitation and encouragement to "try the virtue of the word of God" for ourselves (Alma 31:5).

Without diminishing her confidence and joy in compassionate service, that is what I hope Grandma Harris learned before she left.

CHAPTER TWO

The Biblical Setting

Mary and Martha are mentioned in three different settings in the New Testament. Collectively these accounts of the sisters' interactions with the Savior teach lessons that address many of our daily conflicts and frustrations. Because both women had fervent faith in Christ, their differing personalities and talents can be observed from other angles instead of hierarchically, in order to label one as better than the other. Additionally, consideration of the Savior's teachings before and after His visits with Mary and Martha create a larger context to identify gospel principles.

The sisters receive their biblical introduction well into the final year of the Savior's mortal ministry (Luke 10:38–42). Their encounter with Jesus appears to have transpired soon after the annual Feast of Tabernacles, approximately five to six months before the Savior's crucifixion.

PROPOSED CHRONOLOGY FOR SELECTED EVENTS DURING THE FINAL SIX MONTHS OF THE SAVIOR'S MINISTRY

Because none of the Four Gospels contains every recorded event in Christ's ministry and none is necessarily written in strict chronological order, various chronologies of the Savior's mortal life are available. The accompanying time line establishes the setting for some events surrounding Christ's interaction with Mary and Martha.

	MATTHEW	MARK	LUKE	JOHN
OCTOBER				
Feast of Tabernacles				7:2–13
Teaches the Father's doctrine			7:11–18	
If any man thirst, come				7:37–38
I am the Light				8:12
Parable of the good Samaritan		10:25–27		
First visit to **Mary and Martha**				
in Bethany			10:38–42	
DECEMBER				
Feast of Dedication				10:22–39
Perean ministry				
Parable of the unprofitable				
servant			17:5–10	
Ten lepers healed			17:11–19	

	MATTHEW	MARK	LUKE	JOHN
Returns to Bethany to				
raise Lazarus				11:1–53
Rich young ruler	19:16–26			
Parable of laborers in				
the vineyard	20:1–16			
MARCH				
Mary anoints Jesus' feet				
at Simon's house	26:6–13	14:3–9		12:1–12
Passover				
Week of the Savior's atoning				
sacrifice	21–28	11–16	19–24	12–20

THE FEAST OF TABERNACLES

The Feast of Tabernacles was one of three feasts during the year that the law of Moses commanded all Israelite men to "appear before the Lord . . . in the place which he shall choose" (Deuteronomy 16:16), typically at the temple or its representation. A most joyous celebration, the Feast of Tabernacles lasted eight days, commemorating the gathering in of the year's bounteous harvest (Exodus 23:16) and the wilderness sojourn of the children of Israel.

By the time the Savior was born, additional ceremonies of the Feast of Tabernacles included pouring water from the pool of Siloam on the temple altar and lighting the four fifty-foot candelabra in the temple's Court of the Women, creating an impressive illumination for miles around. These ceremonies reminded participants that without water and without light, no harvest would be produced. In other words, they may plant and apply water to those plants, but in a harsh climate where a good crop depended on favorable weather, the Feast of Tabernacles acknowledged that God gives the increase (see 1 Corinthians 3:6).

Amid the festivities in the year He visited Mary and Martha, Jesus bore witness of Himself in ways that alluded to these ceremonies. For example, relative to the Siloam libation, He taught, "If any man thirst, let him come unto me, and drink. He that believeth on me, as the scripture hath said, out of his belly shall flow rivers of living water" (John 7:37–38). In powerful contrast to the impressive illumination from the candelabra, Jesus declared, "I am the light of the world: he that followeth me shall not walk in darkness, but shall have the light of life" (John 8:12).

During a time when many in Jerusalem expressed division and confusion over the Savior's identity, Jesus taught how they could know for themselves who He was: "If any man will do his will, he shall know of the doctrine, whether it be of God, or whether I speak of myself" (John 7:17). Putting action to faith by coming to Him to drink, following Him through the darkness, and living what He teaches would eliminate any confusion about His identity. Were these the teachings that shaped Mary and Martha's expectations when the Savior visited them in Bethany?

Christ's parable of the good Samaritan appears in the Gospel of Luke immediately before Mary and Martha are introduced. The lawyer's questions that elicited the parable, "What shall I do to inherit eternal life?" and "Who is my neighbour?" (Luke 10:25, 29), echo Christ's Feast of Tabernacles sermons on faith with action. Professed belief is not enough; the Savior invites the lawyer to feed, shelter, and care for anyone who stands in need. Did Mary and Martha hear this parable? How would they have personally internalized the principle?

AT MARTHA'S HOUSE

Shortly after the Feast of Tabernacles, Jesus went to Martha's home in Bethany to teach His gospel. The honor Mary and Martha showed Jesus indicates that this was not their first encounter with Him. Luke 10:39 further implies that the women were already disciples: "And [Martha] had a sister called Mary, which *also sat at Jesus' feet,* and heard his word" (emphasis added). Because this statement is still part of the introduction to the sisters, we gather that both women had previously been taught by the Master. Bethany is a scant two miles east of Jerusalem on the other side of the Mount of

Olives. The proximity of Mary and Martha to where Jesus was teaching during the feast days would have afforded the sisters multiple occasions to hear Him.

The passage begins, "Now it came to pass, *as they went,* that he entered into a certain village" (Luke 10:38; emphasis added), indicating that Jesus was most likely in company with the Twelve when He was welcomed into Martha's home in Bethany. The sisters' expressions of joy at having the Savior in their midst reflect a significant difference between the women. Mary sat at the Savior's feet, listening to His teachings. Martha focused on what is generally assumed to be preparation of food for her guests, although her specific service is unnamed.

THE FEAST OF DEDICATION

Christ returned to Jerusalem during the Feast of Dedication (John 10:22–23). Also called the Festival of Lights, or Hanukkah, this feast was initiated centuries after Moses and celebrated each December to commemorate the rededication of the temple altar after Antiochus IV desecrated it in 166 B.C. A group of Jews surrounded Jesus at the temple and inquired: "How long dost thou make us to doubt? If thou be the Christ, tell us plainly." To which Jesus responded, "I told you, and ye believed not. . . . My sheep hear my voice, and I know them, and they follow me" (John 10:24–27). Again He

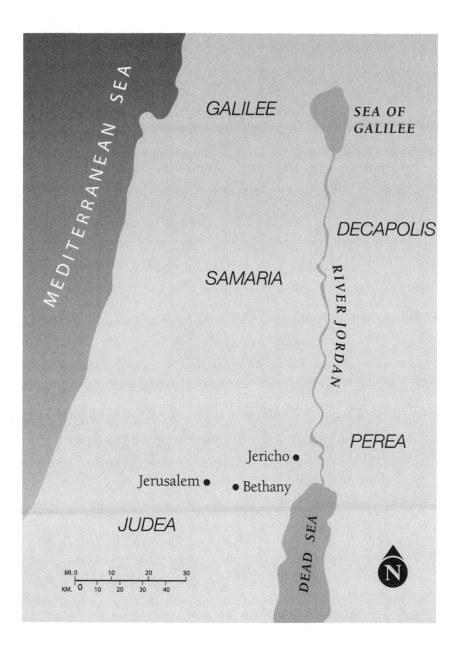

The Holy Land at the time of Christ

reinforced the importance of doing, of living, of following by showing faith through action.

HIS MINISTRY IN PEREA

During the remaining three months that led up to Passover (and to the Savior's crucifixion), Jesus traveled to Perea, on the east bank of the Jordan, some twenty to twenty-five miles east of Jerusalem. During His ministry there, Jesus challenged His listeners to deeper discipleship with teachings underscoring pure motives and commitment. The parable of the unprofitable servant (Luke 17:5–10) answered the disciples' request to "increase our faith" by reminding them that we are ever in the Lord's debt, no matter how much we obey. Later, only one of ten healed lepers returned to thank the Lord for His mercy, prompting the Savior to express disappointment when we fail to acknowledge His service in our lives. "Were there not ten cleansed? but where are the nine? There are not found that returned to give glory to God, save this stranger" (Luke 17:17–18).

The rich young ruler likely encountered the Savior during His Perean ministry (Matthew 19:16–26; Mark 10:17–27; Luke 18:18–27). Reflecting a checklist mentality, the young man asked, "What good thing shall I do, that I may have eternal life?" (Matthew 19:16). When Jesus instructed him to keep the commandments, he replied simply, "Which?" (Matthew 19:18). His confidence in complete compliance since childhood seemed to shatter when Jesus instructed him to give up all his wealth to the poor. What does the commandment not to steal mean when we have all we need? What makes honoring parents a challenging commandment when they provide all we could hope for? By contrast, how different do the commandments appear when we are without status in the community?

Jesus also likely taught the parable of the laborers in the vineyard while in Perea (Matthew 20:1–16). The parable communicates that it isn't how long or where or what we do to serve in the Lord's vineyard but *how* we serve that matters. According to the parable, the Lord will acknowledge our self less service and not skimp on our reward, but He accepts no petty comparison over who helped Him most and who needs His Atonement least.

The Savior was in Perea when Mary and Martha summoned Him with news that their brother Lazarus was seriously ill. Jesus' response provides the second account of His interaction with the sisters (John 11). Timing would prove to be an essential part of this lesson. Jesus purposely delayed His return to arrive in Bethany four days after Lazarus died.

THE MIRACLE OF LAZARUS

Lazarus's body would have been prepared for burial the day of his death, as the Jews of that time did not practice embalming to postpone the body's decomposition. A tradition of care and concern for the body was observed in their burial customs; mourning rituals, including women's wailing and loud expressions of grief, occurred in the days following the burial:

"After death the body was washed, its eyes were closed and its mouth and other orifices were bound shut (Jn 11:44). A mixture of spices was applied to the body, perhaps as a preservation or perhaps to ward off the smell of decomposition for those who visited the tomb later (Jn 11:39; 19:39–40). It was then dressed in its own clothes or placed in a linen shroud (Mt 27:59). Next, a procession, including musicians, family, and (if the family could afford it) professional mourners followed the corpse to the tomb (Mt 9:23). It was customary for mourners to continue to visit the tomb for 30 days, to reanoint the body (Mk 16:1) or to check to be sure the person had not been buried prematurely (Jn 11:31)" (Matthews, *Manners and Customs in the Bible,* 239; see also Brown, *Gospel According to John,* 1:424).

Reflective of the personalities exhibited during their first encounter, Martha hastened to meet Jesus the moment He came into sight. Mary sat still in the house. As soon as Martha met Him, she said, "Lord, if thou hadst been here, my brother had not died" (John 11:21). When Mary first saw Him, "she fell down at his feet, saying unto him, Lord, if thou hadst been here, my brother had not died" (John 11:32). The sisters' statements of confidence in the Savior's power were identical. Both were aware of the many miracles Jesus had performed in Jerusalem. He had restored sight to the blind and health to the infirm, but this miracle would be very different.

Jesus waited for Lazarus to be dead four days. This delay did not merely dispel the Jewish myth that the spirit remained near the lifeless body for three days but, more importantly, gave His disciples something better to believe. In a few weeks' time, Christ's body would be the one that lay in the tomb. Isn't it possible that the Savior engineered this circumstance with Lazarus to teach both male and female disciples that He had power to call His own body back to life? Lazarus was not resurrected on this occasion, but it was as close a circumstance as any to help the disciples appreciate the miracle of resurrection. After four days, the body would have begun to decompose. Martha cried out, "By this time he stinketh," when Jesus ordered the stone cover removed from Lazarus's tomb (John 11:39). But Lazarus came forth whole and very much alive. "I am the resurrection, and the life," Jesus taught on that occasion. "He that believeth in me, though he were dead, yet shall he live" (John 11:25).

During the ensuing weeks, Jesus ministered in Ephraim, Samaria, Galilee, and Perea. But because of the law, He would return to Jerusalem in the spring for Passover—and the Jewish leaders knew He would. So did Mary, Martha, and Lazarus. The third and final scriptural account of the sisters' interaction with Christ took place six days before Passover, at the beginning of the greatest week in history—the week of the Atoning Sacrifice.

AT SIMON'S HOUSE

Jesus was invited to Bethany to dine (John 12:1–9; Matthew 26:6–13; Mark 14:1–9). Martha was again serving, and Mary was again at Jesus' feet. Matthew and Mark identify the event occurring in the home of "Simon the leper." Who was this Simon, and what happened to him in his illness? Such bits of information elicit many more questions than the narrative answers. Consider these possibilities. Is this Simon the father of Martha, Mary, and Lazarus? Is he in attendance at the dinner after Christ healed him from his leprosy? Did his eldest daughter, Martha, act as hostess in the absence of his wife? Or is this the same house that Luke earlier called "Martha's house"? The law of Moses allotted inheritance to daughters only in the absence of sons (Numbers 27:8). In this case, we know that Mary and Martha had a brother, so the home would not be Martha's by inheritance from her father. How then did it become Martha's house? Is she a widow and the house her inheritance bequeathed upon her husband's death? Was Simon Martha's deceased husband? Did Simon die from leprosy? Was this now a dinner of gratitude and celebration for Lazarus's renewed life?

Though the answers to these questions remain a mystery, we are given clues about Mary's and Martha's actions and attitudes during the evening. This time when Jesus came to visit, the concern was not over Martha serving while Mary sat at Jesus' feet. The focus was on the expensive spikenard ointment in an alabaster box that Mary used to anoint Jesus' head and feet. The account reports that Mary's spikenard cost 300 denarii (translated "pence" in the King James Version). Assuming one denarius was payment for a day's labor (Matthew 20:2), Mary's offering represented nearly a year's wages. Ironically, Judas Iscariot was the one to react and complain. He who would betray Jesus to the Jewish leaders in the next day or so for thirty pieces of silver, estimated at 100 denarii, complained over Mary's use of the precious perfume to reverence the Savior. "Mary thought [even this expensive ointment] not good enough to anele Christ's sacred feet," one

biblical scholar observed. "Judas thought a third part of it sufficient reward for selling His very life" (Farrar, *Life of Christ*,
496).

Collectively, these three encounters with Mary and
Martha's family reveal something of their lifestyle and social
class. At least four factors evidence the family's affluence. First,
they had a home large enough to host a sizable number of
guests. Second, though covering a dead body under the ground
in an unmarked grave was traditional for the lower classes,
Lazarus was buried in a tomb hewn in rock. Third, Lazarus's
death summoned extensive public response, suggesting the
family was well-known and regarded in the community. Finally,
Mary was able to secure spikenard in an alabaster box, both
expensive items and viewed as excessive by some.

NO RESPECTER OF PERSONS

If we accept the invitation to apply scripture given
anciently to our own circumstances, we must also consider
whether Christ's teachings to Mary and Martha were gender
specific. In other words, did the Savior's message and motive
differ when directed to women rather than to men?

Biblical scholars and students alike have often perceived
that Christ's reaction to women was unprecedented. Jesus has
been described as the "first feminist," a champion of women's

causes and a revolutionary in recognizing women's contribution to His work.

But as I have studied the Mary and Martha texts, I get a different sense from the Savior's reaction to women. I am struck by the normalcy surrounding exchanges between the Lord and the two sisters. No surprise erupts from anyone that the Lord has elected to visit a woman's home to teach His gospel, only a conscientious desire in the hostesses to show appropriate hospitality to an honored guest. When Lazarus fell ill, Mary and Martha did not hesitate to summon the Lord. No apology for infringing on His precious time accompanied the summons nor for the cultural inappropriateness of a woman requesting service from a man. Mary and Martha's instinctive call to Jesus for help was expected, indicating the assurance of a trusted friendship and confidence that He would naturally respond. At Simon's house, Judas Iscariot reacted to the expense of Mary's oil, not to a cultural perception that women are not to presume such intimate access to a man.

Through these examples, Christ championed not a separate cause for women but the cause for all the honest in heart, all those who desire to follow Him. The Lord's great contribution to the sexes was not to glorify the specific greatness of womanhood but to rejoice with each willing heart and mind, regardless of gender or status. He did not ignore women or treat them as doormats, a common occurrence in every era. But neither did He put women on pedestals or call them *more* spiritual or *more* charitable or *more* helpful than men. He responded to His female disciples with the same love and care with which He responded to His apostles and other male disciples. The Savior is no respecter of persons: "He inviteth . . . all to come unto him and partake of his goodness; and he denieth none that come unto him, black and white, bond and free, male and female; and he remembereth the heathen; and all are alike unto God, both Jew and Gentile" (2 Nephi 26:33).

In short, had Mary and Martha been brothers, or a sister and a brother, Christ's response to them would have been the same. These teachings of Jesus are therefore not only for women but for all those who desire the one needful thing.

CHAPTER THREE

*C*umbered about Much Serving

First to her children and later to her grandchildren, Grandma Harris reinforced the value of efficient work by imparting an array of folksy sayings. When we protested serious activity in the morning by promising we would complete our work later, Grandma recited, "Lazy people do their best when the sun is in the west." When she spotted a hole in a sock or a splitting seam in someone's shirt, she quipped, "A stitch in time saves nine." When one of us carried one small item to another floor of the house, she warned, "We'll be held accountable for all our foolish steps. Why don't you look around and find something else to return upstairs while you're at it?" She also quoted her own mother's advice: "Never be idle. If you can't find something to do, tear a hole in your apron and sew it up again." Who knows how many generations of hard-working, multitasking women found strength to face each day's repetitious chores in this manner?

New Testament Martha manifests a similar respect for economy and productivity in her labors when her personality and talents are teased from the biblical text. A willing and gifted hostess, generous, alert to detail, and very active, Martha is a doer, an implementer. We see her actively serving Christ and His disciples (Luke 10), dashing off to meet Jesus as soon as she heard He was coming (John 11), and again serving a gathering of people (John 12). Her name literally means "mistress" or "lady." Whether at her home or Simon's, she is the lady of the house and takes that role seriously. Not surprisingly, when Jesus commands the stone be removed from Lazarus's four-day tomb, it is Martha who cries out, "Lord, by this time he stinketh" (John 11:39). As the principal woman to prepare Lazarus's body for burial, Martha would have carefully wrapped it in linen strips with aloe, myrrh, and other sweet-smelling perfumes. Consequently, she would also be the first offended by decay's foul odor that swallowed her efforts to create sweetness in the face of death.

CUMBERED ABOUT

Different from the later report of Martha's service at Simon's house, Martha was "cumbered about much serving" during Christ's first recorded visit with the sisters of Bethany (Luke 10:40). The Greek word translated "cumbered" means being pulled in different directions, preoccupied, and distracted. Likely, she wanted to listen to the Lord, but her commitment to service dragged her away from Him to focus on the task at hand.

Over the years, many have criticized Martha for her attention to duty and mismanaged priorities. Knowing Grandma and others like her, I believe Martha would have been hurt and surprised at such criticism. On the contrary, she would have expected praise from us and especially from Jesus. After all, her *much serving* was *for Him,* to show *Him* the depth of her family's respect. In her own way, she wanted to repay Him for His abundance toward them. Out of this sense of gratitude in Martha and Mary's minds, no service could appear too much, no gift excessive.

Can agendas bent on ever accomplishing more become overzealous? The sweetness and peace in service then evaporate, leaving us irritable and dissatisfied. Notice the voice of caution in the Savior's response to Martha's frustration: "Martha, Martha, thou art careful and troubled about many things" (Luke 10:41). The Greek word translated "careful" means being worried, anxious, and full of cares. The Greek word translated "troubled" means bothered by surrounding circumstances or disturbed, as in a crowd of people.

In Zenos's allegory of the olive tree, we note a concern for cumbering things. When he found corrupted fruit on the branches, "the Lord of the vineyard said unto his servant: Let us go to and hew down the trees of the vineyard and cast them into the fire, that they shall not cumber the ground of my vineyard" (Jacob 5:49; see also vv. 44, 66). If left to cumber the ground, the bad would prevent good growth from developing. That happens when branches and roots become unequal (see Jacob 5:48, 66, 73–74).

"Our personal vineyards become lofty and produce strange fruits when we polish only the 'outer vessel' of our lives and allow the 'inner' to rot away," Elder Carlos E. Asay taught in conjunction with the allegory. "I refer to people who perform religious rituals to receive the acclaim of congregations rather than the approval of conscience. I refer to those who become so immersed in administrative and management affairs that they have little time to read, pray, and ponder over the affairs of God. Such persons allow the branches to overcome the roots in their lives." Elder Asay did not stop there. He observed cumbering problems that result by reacting to Martha's weakness with a fanatical approach to Mary-isms. "In contrast," he said, "there are those who invest themselves solely in the books and dig for facts without using their knowledge to bless others. These ever-searching but never-applying souls permit their roots to overrun their branches" ("Rooted and Built Up in Christ," in *Old Testament and the Latter-day Saints*, 13).

When Martha's service became cumbered, it introduced contention and threatened the goodwill offered by the Savior's visit. Most of us have experienced those anxious, troubling emotions when all of our best efforts seem to vanish in our attempt to do more than time and capacity can sustain. We say we are just trying to help, but our conflicting emotions betray us. For example, what happens to peace and fulfillment when I keep my family waiting at home by again working late at the office? What is my source of satisfaction when I spend more time thinking about and creating visual aids for my lesson than preparing meaningful content? What drives my commitment to attend every church function at the expense of caring for a loved one? When does charitable service metamorphose into cumbering service? What is wrong with being cumbered about much service?

THE FOCUS ON ME, THE SERVANT

For starters, cumbered service skews our focus. When our efforts to help are excessive, the focus is on me, the servant, rather than on those to be helped or the enabling power of the

Lord. Martha complained to Jesus, "Dost thou not care that [I am left] to serve alone?" (Luke 10:40). When cumbered about much serving, we see only what we are doing and are blind to another's contribution. As such, we become superb givers but poor receivers. We can't lose ourselves in service to others, then, until we wholeheartedly acknowledge that we can't do it all and graciously receive.

Jesus taught that lesson at the Last Supper while washing the Apostles' feet. "For I have given you an example, that ye should do as I have done to you," the Lord explained to them. "Verily, verily, I say unto you, The servant is not greater than his lord; neither he that is sent greater than he that sent him" (John 13:15–16). In other words, by washing their feet, Jesus wanted His disciples to remember that they were not above the opportunity to serve, even in the most humbling tasks. This is the type of lesson that would make Martha shine. She would be the blue ribbon winner in foot washing, performing above and beyond what most people would imagine. When Jesus says, "Go, and do thou likewise," Martha would find a way to exceed the standard (Luke 10:37).

The context of the incident, however, provides a second reason for this service. Peter objected to the Savior's offer, saying, "Lord, dost thou wash *my* feet?" (John 13:6; emphasis added). Why would Peter object to the Savior's proffered gift?

Because the scripture does not explicitly answer that question, consider possibilities by imagining the Savior offering us the same service. Why might I object to Christ washing my feet?

First, I would protest that I'm not worthy for Him to serve me in that way. I would feel much more comfortable if He would allow *me* to wash *His* feet. This exchange would be appropriate, I could reason, only if I were the servant. Second, I may object because this is one job I think I can do myself. I am fully capable of washing my own feet; no one else is needed for that task. And finally, I may object because of a private concern—my feet are dirty. I'm embarrassed to let the Lord see how filthy I am. Out of respect for Him, I prefer to hide my uncleanness. Perhaps if I could first wash my feet, then I could accept His offer.

But Jesus told Peter, "If I wash thee not, thou hast no part with me" (John 13:8).

What else is Jesus teaching here? Some things—the essential things—we cannot do ourselves. We must let go and allow Christ to come to us. Our attempts at self-purification are superficial treatments at best. Only He can make us clean. When Peter figured it out, he gladly welcomed Christ's selfless service and declared, "Lord, not my feet only, but also my hands and my head" (John 13:9). In essence, Christ was teaching that we need to freely uncover our filth before Him and welcome His cleansing power as the only true covering. His Atonement is therefore not merely a convenient way to be cleansed; it is the only way.

In various settings, the Savior taught Peter, Martha, and us that He came to serve, not to be served (see Matthew 20:28; Mark 10:45). The focus is rightfully on Him.

CAN WE EVER PAY BACK THE LORD?

A second danger in cumbered service is the false belief that after scores of good deeds, we can pay off our debt to Christ. Occasionally I see this confusion in newly called missionaries who observe the tremendous sacrifice they are making to serve a full-time mission. "After all Christ has done for me," they say, "these two years allow me to finally pay Him back." Anyone who has honorably completed a full-time mission will likely recoil at the mere suggestion of payback. They see themselves even deeper in debt to the Lord after their blessings have been exponentially multiplied in His service.

The Book of Mormon leader King Benjamin knew this truth when he taught, "If ye should serve him with all your whole souls yet ye would be unprofitable servants" (Mosiah 2:21). According to King Benjamin, we are indebted to the Lord, owing Him our very lives, because He created us and because he immediately blesses us as payment when we keep

His commandments. "And ye are still indebted unto him, and are, and will be, forever and ever; therefore, of what have ye to boast?" (Mosiah 2:23–24).

Cumbered service twists our perspective to believe that we have finally done enough, so we balk when, inevitably, more is requested. Enlightening in this regard is Christ's parable of the unprofitable servant, in which He queried, "Which of you, having a servant plowing or feeding cattle, will say unto him by and by, when he is come from the field, Go and sit down to meat?" (Luke 17:7). At dinnertime, the servant's role doesn't change simply because he or she earlier did what the Master required. Instead, when the servant returned from completing his work in the fields, the Master would more likely say to him, "Make ready wherewith I may sup, and gird thyself, and serve me, till I have eaten and drunken; and afterward thou shalt eat and drink" (Luke 17:8). Jesus then asked, "Doth he thank that servant because he did the things that were commanded him? I [think] not. So likewise ye, when ye shall have done all those things which are commanded you, say, We are unprofitable servants: we have done that which was our duty to do" (Luke 17:9–10).

In analyzing this parable, Elder John K. Carmack of the Seventy underscored our complaints when we mistakenly assume a release from responsibility to God after completing an act of service. "Too often we allow ourselves to think or even say words like these: 'I don't deserve this setback. You'd think after all I've done, it would not have to be like this. Why must I prove myself over and over again? This is my time to rest from all this responsibility. I've done enough.'"

Elder Carmack explained why we are still in the Lord's debt, even when we have faithfully served Him in the past: "Though the insistence on preparing the meal after a long day of work sounds harsh and ungrateful on its face, in reality that servant is greatly indebted to his master and will always be. . . . No matter how difficult and impossible the circumstances we face, we must retain the attitude that we are still in the Lord's debt. Just keeping the commandments, while laudable, may be enough to maintain our faith but not enough to increase it. We must continue sacrificing and serving with no thought of reward. We do it out of love and gratitude for the Lord, to whom we owe everything" ("Lord, Increase Our Faith," 56).

When our faith and loyalty to the Lord are steadfast and immovable, we do not weary in service to Him.

Elder James E. Talmage shared the "parable of the grateful cat" as an illustration of our ill-placed attempts to pay off our debt to the Savior:

During his daily walk, a naturalist encountered two boys with a basket near the edge of a pond. "In the basket were three whining kittens; two others were drowning in the pond; and the mother cat was running about on the bank, rampant in her distress." In response to the naturalist's inquiry, the boys respectfully explained that they were drowning the kittens per their mistress's instructions, because she wanted only the mother cat, her "particular pet," around the house.

After assuring the boys that he was a friend of their employer and would be responsible for "any apparent dereliction in their obedience" to her orders, the naturalist gave each boy a coin in exchange for the three living kittens. The mother cat seemed to immediately recognize the naturalist as her kittens' deliverer. "As he carried the kittens she trotted along— sometimes following, sometimes alongside, occasionally rubbing against him with grateful yet mournful purrs." He provided appropriate quarters for the kittens at his home, and the mother cat appeared filled with joy.

The following day, the naturalist hosted a "notable company" who had come to honor him. During this genteel affair, in walked the mother cat—carrying in her mouth "a large, fat mouse, not dead, but still feebly struggling under the pains of torturous capture." She deposited the "expiring prey at the feet of the man who had saved her kittens." Elder Talmage's application is poignant:

"What think you of the offering, and of the purpose that

prompted the act? A live mouse, fleshy and fat! Within the cat's power of possible estimation and judgment it was a superlative gift. To her limited understanding no rational creature could feel otherwise than pleased over the present of a meaty mouse. . . .

"Are not our offerings to the Lord—our tithes and our other freewill gifts—as thoroughly unnecessary to His needs as was the mouse to the scientist? But remember that the grateful and sacrificing nature of the cat was enlarged, and in a measure sanctified, by her offering.

"Thanks be to God that He gauges the offerings and sacrifices of His children by the standard of their physical ability and honest intent rather than by the gradation of His exalted station. . . . Our need to serve God is incalculably greater than His need for our service" ("Parable of the Grateful Cat," 875–76).

In Gethsemane and on the cross, Christ didn't suffer just one drop for me; He did it *all* for me. We are infinitely and uniquely blessed by His mercy, merits, and grace. We are miraculously supported and transformed to be more like Him whenever we lose ourselves in His service. No matter how elaborate and plentiful her feast, Martha could not pay back the Lord for His unique gift. Neither can we. On the contrary, all our sincere efforts and desires to serve Him only manifest just how much we desperately need Him.

PRIDE AND PERFECTIONISM

A third destructive influence of cumbered service is the sin of pride, in all its levels of delusion, including perfectionism. With our focus skewed to see only our efforts and the false notion of thereby paying our debt to Christ, we anticipate the praise we will merit for our sacrifice and deeds. In our prideful blindness, we tend to quantify good deeds, concluding the more we daily accomplish, the more like Christ we have become. Within this twisted mind-set evolves the mistaken notion that the more we do and the more we help others, the less we need to draw on help from the Lord. Those who are particularly talented and blessed with multiple gifts may be the most vulnerable to relying on their intellect and skills instead of turning to Christ for strength.

In a revelation to Joseph Smith, the Lord cautioned those who boast of their works after receiving divine assistance:

"The works, and the designs, and the purposes of God cannot be frustrated, neither can they come to naught. . . .

"For although a man may have many revelations, and have power to do many mighty works, yet if he boasts in his own strength, and sets at naught the counsels of God, and follows after the dictates of his own will and carnal desires, he must fall and incur the vengeance of a just God upon him" (D&C 3:1–4).

Taking pride in our accomplishments rather than humbly acknowledging the Lord's enabling power is reflected in the term "*self*-righteousness." In 1913, the First Presidency of the Church warned members of destructive consequences that often follow such arrogance: "People who pride themselves on their strict observance of the rules and ordinances and ceremonies of the Church are led away by false spirits, who exercise an influence so imitative of that which proceeds from a Divine source that even these persons, who think they are 'the very elect,' find it difficult to discern the essential difference" (Smith, Lund, and Penrose, "Warning Voice," 1148).

The Book of Mormon antichrist, Korihor, appears to have been blinded by this genre of pride. He promoted unaided achievement through a person's intellect, brawn, and organizational skills as the necessary source of true success. His humanistic preaching included these assumptions: "Every man fared in this life according to the management of the creature; therefore every man prospered according to his genius, and that every man conquered according to his strength," leading him to conclude that the people had no need for Christ and His Atonement (Alma 30:17).

The effect upon the people was startling: "And thus

[Korihor] did preach unto them, leading away the hearts of many, . . . yea, leading away many women, and also men, to commit whoredoms" (Alma 30:18). The scriptural listing of women before men in this last verse is curious. Without reading too much into it, we can at least conclude that Korihor's influence was not restricted to men. Women were clearly not exempt and maybe even particularly attracted to Korihor's "management of the creature" philosophy.

Quantifying our self-worth by the level of excellence in our good deeds often produces self-doubt. Cumbered service can therefore invite feelings of discouragement that our efforts and accomplishments are never good enough. In our society of abundance and luxury, perfectionism becomes not only a possibility but a well-known reality. The Martha part of us will resonate with one woman's "confessions of a perfectionist," in which she defined a happy life as having her home "completely organized (not one thing out of place) and clean all the time. I wanted my family to pick up after themselves and be on time to all their obligations. I wanted the children to do their homework and come to family scripture study without complaining. I wanted to adhere to a strict schedule and not deviate from it. Early to bed, early to rise. Discipline! I didn't need expensive, new things—I just wanted the possessions I had stewardship over to be in perfect condition." When her friend reacted with "Really?

You just described my hell," the woman was stunned into reevaluating goals that now sounded eerily like Satan's plan of force (Allen-Pratt, "Confessions of a Perfectionist," 65).

King Benjamin counseled his people to serve with "wisdom and order" and to be diligent without excess zeal. "For it is not requisite that a man should run faster than he has strength," he advised. "And again, it is expedient that he should be diligent, that thereby he might win the prize; therefore, all things must be done in order" (Mosiah 4:27). How do the slippery slopes of being "cumbered about much serving" rob us of wisdom and transform order into contention?

Perhaps after hearing Christ's parable of the good Samaritan, Martha chose to welcome the Savior into her home with the greatest display of hospitality. But she seems to have quickly discovered that her plan required more than she had the ability to produce. Figuratively speaking, she had all the burners on the stove going strong as the oven buzzer announced that the baked goods were ready and the greens were wilting—and no one seemed aware of her crisis. She became frustrated, short on patience, and sorely disappointed.

OUR MOTIVATION TO SERVE

Not surprisingly, the Savior supplied Martha with the answer: "One thing is needful" (Luke 10:42). The profound power of simplicity is implied in His response. But "simple" means different things to each of us. In the case of Martha, scholars have long argued the meaning of the one needful thing. Some contend that Jesus is merely telling Martha to prepare one dish rather than a smorgasbord for her guests. Such a response, however, trivializes the story's intent and ignores the underlying problem. One dish to prepare for a meal, one article to write per semester, one project to manage at a time, or one client to serve in a day may be plenty to challenge some of us.

Others are actually more effective, more at peace, and happier when they can do two or more projects simultaneously. President Gordon B. Hinckley addressed women of the Relief Society as "you marvelous women who have chosen the better part." His remarks did not define "the better part" as either a Mary-life or a Martha-life. On the contrary, President Hinckley acknowledged the diversity in the women's ages, situations, and challenges. He counseled, "May you live with love one for another. May you reach down to lift up those whose burdens are heavy. . . . Walk with pride. Hold your heads up. Work with diligence. Do whatever the Church asks you to do. Pray with faith. You may never know how much good you accomplish" (*Ensign,* November 2003, 113, 115).

Choosing the "better part" is therefore remaining steadfast in Christ regardless of our circumstances, challenges, or talents. It is neither what Martha was specifically doing nor what Mary was specifically doing. The better part is finding the One Needful Thing.

The standard is not found in our output but in our motives. Our temperament and focus are telling indicators of when we cross the line from selfless service to cumbered serving. Therefore, the "one needful thing" also takes into account why we serve.

Elder Dallin H. Oaks discussed six reasons to serve that vary in their degree of nobility. He identified the least noble motivation as earthly reward, followed by good companionship, fear of punishment, duty or loyalty, hope for an eternal reward, and finally charity. Pertaining to the highest motivation for service, charity or Christ's love in us, Elder Oaks explained:

"If our service is to be most efficacious, it must be unconcerned with self and heedless of personal advantage. It must be accomplished for the love of God and the love of his children. . . . [From this principle] we learn that it is not enough to serve God with all of our *might and strength*. He who looks into our hearts and knows our minds demands more than this. In order to stand blameless before God at the last day, we must also serve him with all our *heart and mind*" (*Pure in Heart,* 47–49).

Only when we forget ourselves, what others think of us,

and how others' service compares to our efforts can we appreciate and internalize the one needful thing. Only when efforts are motivated by love and selflessness can His peace and gracious Spirit rest within us. Accepting Christ's enabling power is not a weakness—it is our only strength. When we come to Christ, with diligent service born of a pure heart and no thought of reward, we find the One Needful Thing, in all His powerful accessibility.

CHAPTER FOUR

Condemning Another's Service

Doing the weekly laundry was a major chore in Grandma's day. The "wash cycle" required hauling water from the well, heating it in a boiler on a coal-burning stove, and adding a can of lye to soften the water. Next, Grandma skimmed the minerals from the water, added a bar of dissolving P&G laundry soap, and dumped the prepared water into the Maytag washer. She started with the whites so they could be the first to enter the Dexter twin tubs for rinsing—one tub filled with warm rinse water and the other containing bluing. Light colors, dark colors, and finally rugs were sequentially sent through the same water and the same cycle. Finally, Grandma fed each article of clothing through the wringer to be finally hung on the clothesline—where all the neighbors could see.

A clothesline hung with freshly laundered and sorted

clothing on Monday morning sent a message to the world that here lived an efficient, hard-working woman. In Grandma's neighborhood, it meant even more, with enviable stakes indeed. A silent competition raged each week to identify the woman who displayed her clean laundry *earliest* each Monday morning. My mother remembers times when Grandma hustled to have her first load of laundry on the line by 5:30 A.M. only to discover the victory sheets and pillowcases waving on the neighbor's line. "She must have run a batch on Sunday night," Grandma muttered accusingly in her attempt to remain competitive.

COMPETITION OVER OUR DIFFERENCES

When our abilities, possessions, and temperaments are visibly different from those of our neighbor, we inevitably compare. They have a newer car, we have a bigger yard, she requires less sleep, he has more stamina, he is more patient, she is more knowledgeable—or she can do the laundry faster. But most of us rarely stop there. Somehow the word *better* slips into the comparison, explicitly or by our tone of voice, to make it a competition.

Side A: "She's a working mother, but I chose to stay home with my kids."

Side B: "I'm getting an education, so I can be a better mother to my kids."

Side A: "He is still pursuing college degrees, but he should be working to provide and save for his family."

Side B: "He is in a dead-end job because he dropped out of school; I wanted my family to be well-cared for, so we sacrificed for many years so I could get the best education."

From either side of the comparison, condemnation stings. Regardless of which path is chosen, someone will certainly criticize that choice. I considered declining future invitations to speak when a woman commented at a "Know Your Religion" lecture, "After hearing you, I felt discouraged because I will never know the scriptures as well. But then I thought, instead of going to school, I chose to follow the prophet—I married and had a family." Without knowing my choices, she had judged me as disobedient and seemed doubly irked that I was happy about it. As I evaluated whether I should accept invitations to speak, I was reminded that I had not embarked on a career path as my first choice but was led to it by a power greater than I.

Because we can easily detect differences between Mary's and Martha's approaches to service, we may unwittingly introduce the unwarranted "better" to the account, exacerbated by a tendency to label one activity good and the other one bad.

What is better for one, however, is not always better for another.

Elder Joseph B. Wirthlin of the Quorum of the Twelve taught:

"The Church is not a place where perfect people gather to say perfect things, or have perfect thoughts, or have perfect feelings. The Church is a place where imperfect people gather to provide encouragement, support, and service to each other as we press on in our journey to return to our Heavenly Father." He acknowledged differences among us: "Each one of us will travel a different road during this life. Each progresses at a different rate. Temptations that trouble your brother may not challenge you at all. Strengths that you possess may seem impossible to another" ("Virtue of Kindness," 28).

The realization that God prepares a personal mission for each of us is a comforting discovery. By our combined yet differing talents, the whole Church is benefited. In His infinite wisdom, God does not direct us all to be accountants, or seamstresses, or doctors, or musicians. "If the whole body were an eye, where were the hearing?" the Apostle Paul wisely observed. "If the whole were hearing, where were the smelling?" (1 Corinthians 12:17). Collectively, with our combined abilities, we accomplish vastly more and minister to a broader span of needs than we ever could by being cookie-cutter images of each other. Presidencies made up of three individuals from differing backgrounds, offering different skills and perceptions while all sharing a love for the Lord, will have significantly farther-reaching influence than they could if all three members reflected the same interests and talents.

"Never look down on those who are less perfect than you," Elder Wirthlin counseled. "Don't be upset because someone can't sew as well as you, can't throw as well as you, can't row or hoe as well as you.

"We are all children of our Heavenly Father. And we are here with the same purpose: to learn to love Him with all our heart, soul, mind, and strength, and to love our neighbor as ourselves" ("Virtue of Kindness," 28). Instead of futile endeavors to meet the world's impossible expectations, therefore, we are blessed to graciously contribute gifts that God granted to us and focus on the One Needful Thing.

RANKING OUR DIFFERENCES IN SERVICE

Returning to Martha's home in Bethany, we find no hint that Jesus expected, required, or requested any specific service or form of hospitality when He visited the sisters.

"Now it came to pass, as they went, that he entered into a certain village: and a certain woman named Martha received him into her house.

Jesus at the House of Martha and Mary, by Gustave Doré

"And she had a sister called Mary, which also sat at Jesus' feet, and heard his word.

"But Martha was cumbered about much serving, and came to him, and said, Lord, dost thou not care that my sister hath left me to serve alone? bid her therefore that she help me.

"And Jesus answered and said unto her, Martha, Martha, thou art careful and troubled about many things:

"But one thing is needful: and Mary hath chosen that good part, which shall not be taken away from her" (Luke 10:38–42).

Whose idea was it to serve much? Who found a problem in the current situation? Again, this story has much more to do with our attitudes and motives than it has with what we actually do in service. Martha alone detects a problem with her accusation, "Lord, dost thou not care that my sister hath left me to serve alone?" Her complaint is not only towards her sister; Martha accuses the Savior of not caring, of not acknowledging her hard work. Closer scrutiny of the phrase and verb tense suggests that Martha is noting a pattern in Mary's behavior, as if to say, "Mary has abandoned me in the midst of service before; this isn't the first time I've been left to serve alone" (see O'Rahilly, "Two Sisters," 69). In other words, Martha was digging up Mary's past offenses, too.

Perhaps intensified by the sisters' individual responses to

Christ's teaching in the parable of the good Samaritan to "go, and do thou likewise" (Luke 10:37), Martha is zealous about her selected mode of service in contrast to Mary's. And where there is difference, we find a natural inclination to compare and assign relative value. If one is good, the other must be bad, or at least not as good. Likewise, Grandma Harris admitted her prejudice toward her own children. She used to say, "Every old crow thinks hers are the blackest." So when her little girl came home from school complimenting a classmate as "so cute" or "so smart," Grandma would immediately interject, "She can't hold a candle to you!"

Why does a compliment to one have to diminish the value of another? I love the King James Translation of Christ's answer to Martha: "Mary hath chosen that good part, which shall not be taken away from her" (Luke 10:42). What is He saying about Mary's choice of service? It is good. What does that say about Martha's service? Nothing. When we label Martha's active service as not as good, or even bad in comparison to Mary's studious service, we create a dichotomy that Christ did not imply.

Brigham Young University English professor Catherine Corman Parry was spot on in her delightful assessment of the scene:

"Those of us with more of Martha than of Mary in us have

long felt that this rebuke is unjust. While we do not doubt the overriding importance of listening to the Lord, does the listening have to be done during dinner preparations? Would it have hurt Mary to have joined us in serving, then we all could have sat down to hear the Lord together? And furthermore, what about the value of our work in the world? If it weren't for us Marthas cleaning whatever we see and fussing over meals, there would be a lot of dirty, hungry people in this world. . . . Why, oh, why couldn't the Lord have said, 'You're absolutely right, Martha. What are we thinking of to let you do all this work alone? We'll all help, and by the way, that centerpiece looks lovely'?

"What he did say is difficult to bear, but perhaps somewhat less difficult if we examine its context. . . . The Lord acknowledges Martha's care: 'Martha, Martha, thou art careful and troubled about many things' (v. 41). Then he delivers the gentle but clear rebuke. But the rebuke would not have come had Martha not prompted it. The Lord did not go into the kitchen and tell Martha to stop cooking and come listen. Apparently he was content to let her serve him however she cared to, until she judged another person's service: 'Lord, dost thou not care that my sister hath left me to serve alone? bid her therefore that she help me' (v. 40). Martha's self-importance, expressed through her judgment of her sister, occasioned the Lord's rebuke, not her busyness with the meal" ("Simon, I Have Somewhat to Say unto Thee," 116).

GO TO THE ONE WHO HAS OFFENDED US

In addition to accusing the Lord of not caring and condemning Mary for failing to support her service agenda, Martha highlights another problem that often occurs with judgmental service. She is no longer talking to Mary. Martha's accusation is against her sister, but she doesn't tell that to Mary. Instead, Martha goes to Jesus. Why do we seek another's validation in a difference of opinion if not to garner support for our side? Our defense is even better if that person is viewed as an "authority."

During visits to the Church auxiliary offices as a member of the Young Women General Board, I heard secretaries taking calls from ward and stake YW presidents around the country. Frequently, those calls involved a dilemma that went something like this: "Our ward Young Women want to do such and such for an activity/project/experience, but our bishop says he doesn't feel it's appropriate. I think it perfectly fits under this particular YW value. What is the Church's policy on this?" The phone call was loaded with much more than a simple request for policy. Most callers hoped to persuade "an authority" at Church headquarters to say that the YW president was correct so the message could be relayed to the bishop that he was wrong. Fortunately, the secretaries were wise to the trap and helped callers see a higher principle. Greater communication, understanding, and appreciation between auxiliary and priesthood leaders resulted, and YW activities were planned with clearer vision.

As a requirement for sincere discipleship, the Savior taught us to work out our differences directly with the person involved. "Moreover if thy brother [or sister] shall trespass against thee, go and tell him his fault between thee and him alone: if he shall hear thee, thou hast gained thy brother" (Matthew 18:15). Remarkable outcomes result when we follow this counsel.

If we offend someone and that person says nothing of it to neighbors or fellow ward members but straightforwardly comes to us to explain how our words or actions were hurtful, the offended one presents us with the kindest of gifts. In most instances, the offense was never intended. In a moment of carelessness, we said or did something that hurt another. By hearing of our offense openly from the one offended, we receive the ideal environment to apologize and set the record straight. Facing the fruits of our thoughtlessness also encourages us toward keener sensitivity in the future.

On the other hand, if we actually intended offense, the

encounter presents a call to repentance in a most meaningful way—face-to-face with our enemy. Repentance and making amends are facilitated when only the afflicted person requires our sincere apology and explanation and not the rest of the family or the entire ward. Our homes, neighborhoods, and church communities would reflect significant strengthening and healing if we would choose to follow the Savior's simple counsel.

In the darkest hours of the American Revolution, we find a stirring example of both heeding and disregarding this principle. Throughout the war, George Washington's closest confidant was his trusted and indispensable secretary, Joseph Reed. In November 1776, Reed's confidence in Washington became shaken after the commander in chief showed recurring indecision in response to the British threat at New York and Fort Washington.

Rather than communicating these fears to Washington directly, Reed secretly exposed them in a letter dated 21 November to Major General Charles Lee, Washington's second in command, and now Reed's choice as most qualified leader.

"I do not mean to flatter or praise you at the expense of any other," Reed wrote to Lee, "but I confess I do think it is entirely owing to you that this army, and the liberties of

America . . . are not totally cut off. . . . You have decision, a quality often wanted in minds otherwise valuable. . . . All circumstances considered, we are in a very awful and alarming situation—one that requires the utmost wisdom and firmness of mind. As soon as the season will admit, I think yourself and some others should go to Congress and form the plan of the new army" (McCullough, *1776*, 248–49).

Lee's response arrived by express rider some nine days later in a sealed envelope addressed to Reed. Because Reed was absent and Washington was anxiously awaiting news of Lee's whereabouts, he tore open the letter and read the devastating contents addressed to "My dear Reed":

"I received your most obliging, flattering letter—lament with you that fatal indecision of mind which in war is a much greater disqualification than stupidity or even want of personal courage. Accident may put a decisive blunder in the right, but eternal defeat and miscarriage must attend the men of the best parts if cursed with indecision" (McCullough, *1776*, 254).

After reading the contents of the letter, Washington could deduce the other half of the conversation and thereby concluded that both his secretary and his second in command had lost faith in him. His reaction to such traumatizing news is laudable and instructive. Resealing the letter to be sent on to Reed, Washington added a note of explanation, before

graciously thanking Reed for his efforts during his present journey and wishing him a successful mission:

"The enclosed was put into my hands by an express [rider].
. . . Having no idea of its being a private letter . . . I opened it.
. . . This, as it is the truth, must be my excuse for seeing the
contents of a letter which neither inclination *or* intention
would have prompted me to" (McCullough, *1776,* 255).

"Possibly, Washington was more hurt than angry," historian
David McCullough surmised of Washington's subsequent
emotional state. In a later conversation with Reed, Washington
would explain, "I was hurt not because I thought my judgment
wronged by the expressions contained in it [the letter], but
because the same sentiments were not communicated immediately to myself" (McCullough, *1776,* 255). History records
that Reed's loyalties returned squarely to Washington's corner,
never again to waver. But at what a price Washington offered
the olive leaf with pure nobility of character and complete for-
giveness.

Like Martha, we would all do well to "go and tell [our sister her] fault" between us two alone and allow two hearts to
become knit together in love and greater understanding.
Accepting the Lord's counsel, we will contribute much
through our combined efforts to serve the Lord and follow the
example of the good Samaritan. On the other hand, if we

choose to disregard His directive, we compromise an otherwise harmonious environment.

Nineteenth-century Scottish theologian Henry Drummond observed that "the peculiarity of ill temper is that it is the vice of the virtuous. It is often the one blot on an otherwise noble character. You know men who are all but perfect, and women who would be entirely perfect, but for an easily ruffled, quick-tempered or 'touchy' disposition. This compatibility of ill temper with high moral character is one of the strangest and saddest problems of ethics" (*Greatest Thing in the World*, 35).

Classifying sins as either those of the body or those of disposition, Drummond considered the prodigal son in Christ's parable as a type of sins of the body and the elder brother in the parable as a type of sins of disposition. An unrepentant Martha could likewise be perceived as a type of the elder brother without drawing any parallel between the prodigal and Mary. Drummond suggested that "society has no doubt whatever as to which of these [types of sins] is worse. Its brand falls, without a challenge, upon the Prodigal. But are we right?" His evidence for this conclusion is compelling: "No form of vice, not worldliness, not greed of gold, not drunkenness itself, does more to un-Christianize society than evil temper. For embittering life, for breaking up communities; for destroying the most sacred relationships; for devastating homes; for withering up men and women; for taking the bloom of child-hood; in short, for sheer gratuitous misery-producing power, this influence stands alone" (*Greatest Thing in the World,* 35–36).

Returning to the parable, Drummond invited the reader to "analyze, as a study in Temper, the thunder-cloud itself as it gathers upon the Elder Brother's brow. What is it made of? Jealousy, anger, pride, uncharity, cruelty, self-righteousness, touchiness, doggedness, sullenness—these are the ingredients of this dark and loveless soul. In varying proportions, also, these are the ingredients of all ill temper. Judge if such sins of the disposition are not worse to live in, and for others to live with, than sins of the body" (*Greatest Thing in the World,* 36–37).

Citing Jesus in His declaration that publicans and harlots would go to heaven before the malcontented Jewish leaders, Drummond concluded: "There is really no place in heaven for a disposition like this. A man with such a mood could only make Heaven miserable for all the people in it. Except, there-fore, such a man be born again, he cannot, he simply *cannot,* enter the Kingdom of Heaven" (*Greatest Thing in the World,* 37–38).

All the good we might do through fine talents and efficient manner quickly dissolves when we condemn another's service.

By seeing our contribution as essential and another's as inconsequential, by judging one person's act of service as better than another's when both are sincerely offered, and by refusing communication with those we don't understand, we plant seeds of contention and misery in any room we enter.

Martha is noteworthy because she did heed the Savior's message. She changed her perspective without losing her zeal to actively serve. In turn, Martha benefited from different alms offered that evening by others in attendance. Mary's reverent gift, presented at the feet of the Savior, for example, would have filled the home with aromatic reverence and awe for the Holy One of Israel. In consequence, everyone was blessed by Mary's unique offering.

CHAPTER FIVE

$\mathscr{M}$ary's Choice of That Good Part

Mary presents a singular example of Christian discipleship. In all three settings, she is seen at the feet of the Savior. Her awe for Jesus communicates an ability to reverence Him as the Messiah during His mortal ministry, when He had no "comeliness . . . that we should desire him" (Mosiah 14:2; Isaiah 53:2). It is one thing to know in your head that this is the Christ and quite another to have that understanding reverberate in your soul.

During Christ's initial visit with the sisters of Bethany, Mary could have easily been the one judging Martha's service by complaining of her bustling around while she was trying to listen to the Lord. But Mary gives no indication that she even heard Martha's accusation against her. Elder Marvin J. Ashton taught that we should never be offended by someone who is trying to serve the Lord:

"Perhaps the greatest charity comes when we are kind to each other, when we don't judge or categorize someone else. . . . Charity is accepting someone's differences, weaknesses, and shortcomings; having patience with someone who has let us down; or resisting the impulse to become offended when someone doesn't handle something the way we might have hoped" (Tongue Can Be a Sharp Sword," 19).

Mary's purity of motives, simplicity of agenda, and absence of pride attract the Savior's nod of approval, not necessarily what she did to serve Him. Mary's heart, void of offense, is reflected in a thoughtful poem by Shirley Adwena Harvey:

Your dark eyes never left His gentle face
As you sat listening near the Savior's feet
While Martha's hurried steps kept constant pace
With the rhythm of your heart's excited beat.
Your sister's call to serve was never heard,
You gave no thought to feasting or attire—
Your ears were strained to catch each precious word
As spirit burned within you like a fire.
You knew this was the moment you should seek
The needful things to fill your longing heart
And joy-tears must have trickled down your cheek
When He said you had chosen that good part.

Dear Mary, in your sweet, far-sighted way—
You teach us of priorities today.
> ("To Mary—Who Sat at Jesus' Feet," 49;
> used by permission)

SERVICE TO THE LORD THROUGH LISTENING AND LEARNING

Having first identified Mary's pure motives, we can now consider what Mary *did* in service to receive Christ's approval. Without denigrating Martha's contribution, Jesus assigned virtue to Mary's choice of service: "But one thing is needful: and Mary hath chosen that good part, which shall not be taken away from her" (Luke 10:42). What did He say about what Martha was doing? Nothing. What did He say of Mary's choice? "Mary hath chosen that good part." That Mary chose to quietly listen to Christ and His gospel—during dinner preparations—provides additional instruction for consideration.

The custom of the day would have the women serving meals to the men reclined on the floor and afterwards eating their meal by themselves. In traditional settings today, a woman or girl who sits and listens to a gospel discussion while another woman prepares a lavish dinner risks ridicule. She might be called lazy or unfeminine but would not likely be praised for her appropriate use of time. Jesus never requires that we choose one or the other: household duties or gospel study. Daily life requires our attention to both—by men and women alike. Too often, however, spiritual nourishment is swallowed up in the temporal crises of the moment.

As an undergraduate student, I remember hearing Sister Camilla Kimball speak to a large audience of single LDS college women. Her voice rang with certainty when she charged us, "I hope none of you is here at the university just to find a husband! Get a good education—a serious education!" Her charge deeply impressed me at the time because it sounded foreign among all the lessons of marriage preparation and homemaking. Somehow I feared to verbalize academic or studious goals because they were labeled uncomely for a young woman—especially if she ever wanted to marry.

About the same time I heard her husband, President Spencer W. Kimball, quoted as saying, "We want our homes to be blessed with sister scriptorians—whether you are single or married, young or old, widowed or living in a family. . . . Become scholars of the scriptures—not to put others down, but to lift them up" (*Teachings of Spencer W. Kimball,* 321). Later, he counseled young women, "Before you fall in love with a choice young man, fall in love with the scriptures" ("In Love and Power and without Fear," 8). President and Sister Kimball's encouragement to young women in this regard echoed Christ's teachings pertaining to Mary's gospel learning: It is good.

The Savior observed that Mary's service could not be taken from her. Truths learned through study and faith are ours for eternity. Gaining reverence for doctrines and gospel principles through the Spirit's tutelage and daily application will determine our paths tomorrow. As more and more women and men discover scripture enlightenment through personal study, family discussions, full-time missionary service, and Sunday School and other religion classes, families will grow in greater truth and light.

Mary showed us that gospel study can be done even amid the demands and distractions of every day life. She did not let a burgeoning agenda blind her to the one needful thing. She learned to listen and ponder. Her outward calm indicates balance and focus. Addressing young adults, President Gordon B. Hinckley challenged his audience to create balance in life by attending to four obligations: "one's vocation, one's family, the Church, and to one's self." In reference to the final obligation, to one's self, President Hinckley said:

"I decry the great waste of time that people put into watching inane television. . . . I believe their lives would be enriched if, instead of sitting on the sofa and watching a game that will be forgotten tomorrow, they would read and think and ponder." "You need time to meditate and ponder, to think, to wonder at the great plan of happiness that the Lord has outlined for His children. You need time to read. You need to read the scriptures. You need to read good literature. You need to partake of the great culture which is available to all of us" ("Resolve to Keep Balance in Your Lives," 24).

Feminist scholarship has questioned interpretations claiming that women in the Gospels show strength and significant contribution. This perspective charges that Luke's narratives, in particular, promote an agenda to, as they say, restrict and control women by showing them as silent and passive, either performing simple charitable acts or dependent on Jesus (see Reid, *Choosing the Better Part?* 2–14). Such claims see no strength in Mary's sitting at Jesus' feet because Mary is merely listening; she isn't given a voice. Considering Mary's example in a broader context, however, identifies what she ultimately became and what she uniquely contributed *because* she listened and found the one needful thing.

MARY AS A MISSIONARY

The miracle of raising Lazarus from the dead created an excitement and reverence for the Savior previously unknown. The miracle's publicity also invited a serious plan to stop the Master from further notoriety. Chief priests and Pharisees gathered to plan the demise of Jesus and "consulted that they might put Lazarus also to death; because that by reason of him many of the Jews went away, and believed on Jesus" (John 12:10–11). We could easily assume, therefore, that Lazarus would be the chief missionary to spread the news that the Messiah is come: the Holy One of Israel is here with power in His wings. Interestingly, no mention is made of Lazarus as a missionary in this regard. But Mary is.

"And he that was dead came forth, bound hand and foot with graveclothes: and his face was bound about with a napkin. Jesus saith unto them, Loose him, and let him go.

"Then many of the Jews which came to Mary, and had seen the things which Jesus did, *believed on him"* (John 11:44–45; emphasis added).

Mary's audience would not ask questions concerning conditions of being dead for four days before returning to life. Likewise, her ministerial message would not be expected to focus on what occurs in the spirit world after one dies. Mary would rather teach doctrinal truths she learned at the Savior's feet. Her witness, borne of the Spirit, would echo what her inquirers saw and felt in the Master's presence. She became a noteworthy missionary by following the Lord's counsel of preparation:

"Seek not to declare my word, but first seek to obtain my word, and then shall your tongue be loosed; then, if you desire, you shall have my Spirit and my word, yea, the power of God unto the convincing of men.

"But now hold your peace; study my word which hath gone

forth among the children of men, . . . and then shall all things be added thereto" (D&C 11:21–22).

Her gift of listening and pondering enabled her to lead others to Christ and His saving power. Scriptural evidence of Mary's service to the Savior, however, does not end here. Learning at the feet of the Savior prepared Mary for another remarkable, even singular, opportunity to serve the Master.

ANOINTING THE SAVIOR FOR HIS BURIAL

While Martha quietly served the company their supper, doing what she loved to do, Mary was free to share her gift with the Savior. Somehow, somewhere, amid all the opportunities to learn at Jesus' feet, Mary came to accept a truth that apparently no one else on record yet understood. When talk of the Master's death brought denial and defense from other disciples, Mary recognized that His departure was inevitable. Of Mary's early understanding, Elder Bruce R. McConkie taught, "Again Jesus announces that the Lord Jehovah shall die (Isaiah 53:9), and in doing so lets us know that Mary, at least, foreknew and realized what her beloved Lord would soon face" (*Doctrinal New Testament Commentary,* 1:700). Rather than fighting against that truth, Mary sought to sustain the Savior in His greatest mission, for the very purpose He came to earth.

Reflecting her obvious awe for Jesus, Mary presented an

alabaster vial or cruse of pure, undiluted spikenard to anoint His feet and head in acknowledgment of His impending death and subsequent anointing with spices. Alabaster is a translucent stone that can be carved to create beautiful containers. While not uncommon in the ancient Near East, alabaster was nonetheless obtained only at considerable cost. Mark and Matthew report that Mary "brake the box" to release the fragrant oil, suggesting the vial had a narrow neck (Mark 3:14; see also Matthew 26:7). Once opened, it could not be resealed. She would use all of the precious oil to anoint the Lord.

The perfume typically used in burial preparations was myrrh, made from the gummy resin of a balsam tree. But all three Gospel reports of Mary's anointing are impressed that she brought spikenard, "a fragrant oil derived from the root and spike (hair stem) of the nard plant which grows in the mountains of northern India" (Brown, *Gospel According to John,* 1:448).

Mark and Matthew report that Mary anointed Christ's head in preparation for His burial; John tells us she anointed His feet. Throughout the Old Testament, kings and priests were anointed on their heads in connection with a calling to serve (see Exodus 28:41; 1 Samuel 15:1; 16:3; Psalm 23:5). Feet were anointed when the entire body was being prepared for burial. Elder James E. Talmage observed the sacred respect shown by Mary's act:

"To anoint the head of a guest with ordinary oil was to do him honor; to anoint his feet also was to show unusual and signal regard; but the anointing of head and feet with spikenard, and in such abundance, was an act of reverential homage rarely rendered even to kings. Mary's act was an expression of adoration; it was the fragrant outwelling of a heart overflowing with worship and affection" (*Jesus the Christ,* 512).

Because of striking similarities between Mary's anointing, reported in John, Mark, and Matthew, and the sinful woman washing the Savior's feet with her tears, recorded in Luke 7, many have wanted to fuse them as aspects of the same story involving only one woman—Mary of Bethany. Subsequently, nothing precludes them from seeing the same woman in the opening verses of Luke 8 as she from whom seven devils were exorcised, now called Mary Magdalene. Yet the larger scriptural context and consideration of details in the stories require us to see these as separate incidents. Raymond E. Brown, a New Testament scholar, relates the domino effect of meshing these stories together:

"In the popular mind, under the influence of the Lucan picture of a sinful woman, the woman of Bethany (Mary, according to John) was soon characterized as a sinner. Then, for good measure, this sinful Mary of Bethany was identified with Mary of Magdala from whom seven devils had been cast out (Luke viii:2) and who went to the tomb of Jesus. And so, for instance, the Catholic liturgy came to honor in a single feast all three women (the sinner of Galilee, Mary of Bethany, Mary of Magdala) as one saint—a confusion that has existed in the Western Church, although not without demur, since the time of Gregory the Great" (*Gospel According to John,* 1:452).

Though we should not feel consternation that one who becomes an enlightened disciple of Christ was once a publicly known sinner, why should we label a disciple as a grave sinner when there is no evidence of such? The good news of the gospel proclaims that the healing of sick souls is frequent evidence of Christ's all-powerful Atonement. But what good is accomplished by going out of our way to merge three female disciples into one? Seen separately, each one in her turn bears witness of Christ's divinity and power to save. Three individuals in three different circumstances testify of the Lord's power and goodness in their individual cases. The result is three times richer than we would have with only one witness.

It is worthy of note that Jesus responded to Mary's anointing. John tells us that Jesus hushed Judas' protests that the cost of the ointment would be better used for the poor, but He didn't dissuade Mary: "Let her alone: *for she hath preserved this ointment until now, that she might anoint me in token of my burial.* For the poor always ye have with you; but me ye have not always" (JST John 12:7–8; emphasis added). This passage, including insights from the Joseph Smith Translation, further underscores Mary's advanced understanding that Jesus must die because she procured in advance and saved the spikenard for this very purpose.

Mark and Matthew observe yet another manifestation of the Savior's respect for Mary's service. Speaking to those disciples in attendance, Jesus prophesied, "Wheresoever this gospel shall be preached in the whole world, there shall also this, that this woman hath done, be told for a memorial of her" (Matthew 26:13; see also Mark 14:9). The Joseph Smith Translation emphasizes Mary's influence on future generations because of her openness to revelation *before* His death:

"She [Mary] hath done what she could: and this which she has done unto me, shall be had in remembrance in generations to come, wheresoever my gospel shall be preached; for verily she has come beforehand to anoint my body to the burying" (JST Mark 14:8).

The Savior's clear acceptance of Mary's offering reinforces the power of listening, pondering, and learning by the Spirit.

Her service was good because it was dependent on Him and motivated by love for Him. Mary willingly lost herself in service to Christ. She found and accepted the One that is needful, which blessing would not be taken from her.

CHAPTER SIX

Martha's Gracious Response

Latter-day Saints highly esteem hard work and sacrifice. From the Garden of Eden, God cursed the ground for Adam's sake, so that "by the sweat of [our] face" we eat our bread (Moses 4:25; Genesis 3:19). We hear such sage advice as "It's better to give than to receive," "You get what you pay for," and "Strive for self-sufficiency." Admitting that we need others and accepting their help can therefore seem like an admission of weakness and a sign of failure. If we sense success when someone tells us, "You're awfully hard to help," we may learn something from Martha's gracious response.

Only a few months separated Christ's visits to Bethany in Luke 10 and John 12, but during the interim, Martha's attitude and motive in serving changed. Substantiation that she accepted Christ's counsel is evident when, during the later visit, Martha is still the one serving supper to Christ and His disciples, just as she had before, but this time we hardly notice her:

"Then Jesus six days before the passover came to Bethany, where Lazarus was which had been dead, whom he raised from the dead.

"There they made him a supper; and Martha served: but Lazarus was one of them that sat at the table with him.

"Then took Mary a pound of ointment of spikenard . . . and anointed the feet of Jesus. . . .

"Then saith one of his disciples, Judas Iscariot, . . .

"Why was not this ointment sold . . . and given to the poor?" (John 12:1–5).

At this supper, the focus is on Christ—with Mary anointing His feet. In the periphery, we note with interest the presence of Lazarus, recently raised from the dead, and also a disciple who is unhappy with Christ's attention to Mary's service. But this time that disciple who complains is Judas Iscariot, not Martha.

Most scholars assume that this event occurred on Saturday evening, soon after the Sabbath ended. If that were the case, Martha could not have begun dinner preparations until after sunset, making dinner later than usual and adding stress to feeding the large group of visitors. If Martha is therefore easy to miss in the scene, it is a great compliment to her changed heart and genuine delight in service. In contrast to her cumbered and judgmental service the previous October, Martha would now be embarrassed should anyone shower her with exorbitant praise for her efforts, thereby drawing attention away from the Savior. Martha shows no indication of jealousy toward Mary's service or what anyone else was doing. The scene reflects her contentment in selfless service.

DOING ALMS WITHOUT BEING SEEN OF MEN

Many of the disciples, blessed that evening by Martha's service, would have heard the Savior's earlier teachings on quiet service in His Sermon on the Mount:

"Take heed that ye do not your alms before men, to be seen of them: otherwise ye have no reward of your Father which is in heaven.

"Therefore when thou doest thine alms, do not sound a trumpet before thee, as the hypocrites do in the synagogues and in the streets, that they may have glory of men. Verily I say unto you, They have their reward.

"But when thou doest alms, let not thy left hand know what thy right hand doeth:

"That thine alms may be in secret: and thy Father which

seeth in secret himself shall reward thee openly" (Matthew 6:1–4).

In Martha we have a fine example of giving alms without sounding a trumpet. Her service is now rendered without concern for publicity. When our left hand knows what our right hand is doing, the two hands connect; when our two hands collide, we hear applause. Giving service without fanfare, sharing love without need of an audience or public approval, is an essential indication of charity, "the pure love of Christ" (Moroni 7:47). "Though I speak with the tongues of men and of angels, and have not charity," the Apostle Paul taught, "I am become as sounding brass, or a tinkling cymbal" (1 Corinthians 13:1). Charity isn't worried about publicity and would be confused at applause.

B. C. Forbes, founder of *Forbes Magazine,* observed our misplaced concern for public approval: "When we are young— and some of us never get over it—we are apt to think that applause, conspicuousness and fame constitute success. But they are only the trappings, the trimmings. Success itself is the work, the achievement that evokes these manifestations. . . . Concentrate on your work and the applause will take care of itself" (*Reader's Digest,* cover).

President Howard W. Hunter warned of the spiritual dangers associated with serving in order to be in the spotlight.

Martha, Martha, by Elspeth Young

Those so motivated, he said, "may come to covet the notoriety and thus forget the significance of the service being rendered. . . . You must not allow yourselves to focus on the fleeting light of popularity or substitute that attractive glow for the substance of true, but often anonymous labor that brings the attention of God even if it does not get coverage on the six o'clock news. In fact, applause and attention can become the spiritual Achilles' heel of even the most gifted among us" (*Teachings of Howard W. Hunter,* 66).

One wonders at the staggering quantity and quality of service rendered throughout history that only God has noted. Significant contributions that even the brightest record keepers cannot deduce are known and clearly remembered by the Lord. Just before her release as Young Women General President, Ardeth G. Kapp reviewed history books compiled to represent the progress of young women in the Church during her leadership. She reported to her general board that the experience elicited a flood of wonderful memories of contributions made by those highlighted in the books. But the experience also produced memories of many other women and men whose efforts had significantly supported and strengthened young lives during those nearly eight years. Where were these acts of service recorded? Who would remember them?

These questions led her to a new appreciation for the

ubiquitous Book of Mormon phrase: "And it came to pass."
With her new insight, Sister Kapp saw in that phrase a representation of countless disciples who helped move God's work
from where it had been to where it then was. Those names and
acts of service are not announced to us "that [their] alms may
be in secret: and [their] Father which seeth in secret himself
shall reward [them] openly" (Matthew 6:4). The Father's "history book" perfectly remembers each act of service sincerely
rendered.

Not Anonymous Service

Providing service without tinkling cymbals and trumpet
accompaniment, however, does not require that service be
anonymous to the one served. C. Louise Brown, a professional
LDS social worker, observed dysfunctional consequences
when we always hide from those we serve. "Thinking that we
should secretively [serve] because the right hand represents
the giver and the left hand the receiver, . . . we avoid taking
thought for the recipients' feelings or responsibility to assist
them with subsequent needs. On the other hand, . . . we often
sound our trumpets in meetings to those we have not
served. Such a disconnected way of serving keeps givers and
receivers separated from each other in a way that prevents the
development of reciprocal, empathic feelings and relieves both

of any responsibility concerning the gift" ("Walking in the World," 2).

Tender emotions surface when I remember discovering a way to serve Grandma Harris. Because she had given so much to me, I *needed* the chance to reciprocate in a meaningful way. In reality, Grandma gave me one of her finest gifts when she graciously and overtly accepted my help, communicating that my efforts made a difference.

Humble service known to the recipient without broadcasting it to the world is often manifested at funerals. After the death of a loved one, family and friends are frequently amazed at the number of people profoundly touched by the life of one individual. They also acknowledge surprise over the kinds of personalized service their loved one offered, without anyone but the recipient ever knowing. Heaven and earth are very close at such times as we feel the Savior's love and mercy. In the words of a beloved hymn:

> *Each life that touches ours for good*
> *Reflects thine own great mercy, Lord;*
> *Thou sendest blessings from above*
> *Thru words and deeds of those who love.*
>
> *What greater gift dost thou bestow,*
> *What greater goodness can we know*
> *Than Christlike friends, whose gentle ways*
> *Strengthen our faith, enrich our days.*

When such a friend from us departs,
We hold forever in our hearts
A sweet and hallowed memory,
Bringing us nearer, Lord, to thee.
                    (Hymns, *no. 293*)

Serving to impress the public is a far cry from the mutually enriching exchange that occurs as giver and receiver meet and afterwards feel to be the one blessed. With the words "Tell no man" (Luke 5:14), Jesus cautioned those He healed to avoid publicizing to the world the service rendered, but He was never invisible to those He helped. On the contrary, if necessary, He went out of His way to orchestrate an exchange with the one served.

THE SAVIOR AS EXAMPLE

Consider, for example, when the Savior healed the woman of a blood disease she had suffered for twelve years. If anyone wanted anonymity after this service was rendered, it was the woman, not Jesus. Weakened by her anemic condition, the woman hoped merely to touch the hem of His clothing to be healed without His ever registering her presence. "For she said, If I may touch but his clothes, I shall be whole" (Mark 5:28). As a social outcast, she may have been anxious that Christ not be required to heal her by touch, fearing she might thereby render Him unclean. In response to her remarkable faith, "straightway the fountain of her blood was dried up; and she felt in her body that she was healed of that plague" (Mark 5:29).

The Savior, however, would not let her slip away unnoticed. "Jesus . . . turned him about in the press, and said, Who touched my clothes?" (Mark 5:30). He would have giver and receiver meet. When, "fearing and trembling," the woman acknowledged that she had touched Him, Jesus further blessed her, "Daughter, thy faith hath made thee whole" (Mark 5:33–34). With this exchange, does the woman recipient give something to the Lord? Christ as giver was blessed and strengthened by interacting with the one He helped.

Consider the ten lepers who petitioned the Lord to heal them of their tragic disease. In answer to their petition, all ten were healed. But only "one of them, when he saw that he was healed, turned back, and with a loud voice glorified God, and fell down on his face at his feet, giving him thanks" (Luke 17:15–16). Jesus was not embarrassed by this show of appreciation. On the contrary, He wondered why the others did not do the same, saying, "Were there not ten cleansed? but where are the nine?" (Luke 17:17).

During His visit to the Nephites after His resurrection, Jesus Christ blessed an entire multitude one by one (3 Nephi 17:9). This was not anonymous service. He then "commanded

MARTHA'S GRACIOUS RESPONSE

that their little children should be brought" to Him. Surrounded by these little ones, He and all the multitude knelt
upon the earth while He prayed to the Father such "great and
marvelous things" that "no tongue can speak, . . . neither can
the hearts of men conceive" (3 Nephi 17:11, 16–17). The multitude was so filled with great joy at this experience that "they
were overcome." The Savior was also blessed and fortified by
the experience: "Blessed are ye because of your faith. And now
behold, *my joy is full. And when he had said these words, he
wept,* and the multitude bare record of it, and he took their
little children, one by one, and blessed them, and prayed unto
the Father for them" (3 Nephi 17:18, 20–21; emphasis added).
Who is the giver and who is the receiver in this account?

Realizing that we become recipients in the process of serving may explain why we are never really comfortable being
called a "good Samaritan." In reaching out to help others, we
are nourished and strengthened in return. Selfless service suc-
cessfully rendered manifests in the servant both a giving and
an accepting heart. A Christlike servant knows that she never
does all the giving; if she will allow it, the one she serves gives
her much in return. A true servant also graciously receives.

During the Savior's visit to Bethany, scant days before His
mortal ministry concluded, Martha chose to joyfully receive
without losing her talent for giving. She accepted Christ's

gentle counsel not to judge another's service and instead remove cumbrances in her own service. Consequently, Jesus, Mary, Lazarus, and the others present were recipients of Martha's generous yet humble offering. And at the same time, Martha's peaceful service allowed the focus to rightfully center on the only One who is needful.

$\mathscr{P}$riorities: Putting God First

At times we may not want to see Mary and Martha calmly, cheerfully, and harmoniously serving in their unique ways. We may look at all the chaos surrounding our lives and feel we have lost a kindred spirit in Martha transformed. Our society has made an art of being time challenged and given us plenty of justification for being cumbered and fretful. We fear failure if our planners aren't continually filled with appointments and commitments. Distractions become welcome escapes from duty and the "all-that-I-should-be-doing" list. Not surprisingly, prioritizing then becomes a luxury or just one more time-consuming exercise to prevent accomplishment.

To those whom the Lord addressed as "scribes and Pharisees, hypocrites," He gave sharp chastisement for their blindness to priorities. These religious leaders took pride in exact calculations for tithe offerings, including their herbs and spices, while they "omitted the weightier matters" of justice, mercy, and faith (Matthew 23:23; see also D&C 117:8). Some things are clearly more important than others to the Lord. Elder Richard G. Scott of the Twelve has therefore cautioned:

"Are there so many fascinating, exciting things to do or so many challenges pressing down upon you that it is hard to keep focused on that which is essential? When things of the world crowd in, all too often the wrong things take highest priority. Then it is easy to forget the fundamental purpose of life. Satan has a powerful tool to use against good people. It is distraction. He would have good people fill life with 'good things' so there is no room for the essential ones. Have you unconsciously been caught in that trap?" ("First Things First," 7).

Jesus Christ has not left us to discern the weightier matters on our own. A closer look at Luke's account of Christ's first visit with Mary and Martha reveals a pattern. A curious transition among word images emerges from the Savior's teachings when considered in this light. With exquisite economy of words, Jesus leads us from Martha's carefulness about *many things* to only *one thing being needful* to finally choosing *that which cannot be taken away*. One biblical scholar saw this "intentional gradation" as the critical crux of Christ's message: "a numerical diminuendo with a spiritual crescendo; shifting key, if you will, from a quantitative to a qualitative basis" (Gillieson, "Plea for Proportion," 111). Simplifying our temporal environment leads to discovery in the spiritual environment. Finding Christ opens the world we yearn to enter but cannot fathom on our own.

THE KEY TO SETTING PRIORITIES

In numerous ways, the Lord has underscored the key to setting priorities and choosing wisely. God gave Moses ten commandments, but the *first* one was "Thou shalt have no other gods before me" (Exodus 20:3). Joseph Smith identified thirteen articles of our belief, but the *first* one is "We believe in God, the Eternal Father, and in his Son, Jesus Christ, and in the Holy Ghost" (Article of Faith 1). Of all 613 commandments listed by Jewish leaders from the law of Moses, Jesus identified "the *first* and great commandment" to be "Thou shalt love the Lord thy God with all thy heart, and with all thy soul, and with all thy mind" (Matthew 22:38, 37). Captain Moroni's people fought for many righteous causes, but the *first* one listed on the Title of Liberty was "In memory of our God" (Alma 46:12). The ultimate destination attained by pressing forward and clinging to the iron rod in Lehi's dream was the tree of life. And what filled his soul with exceeding great joy when he arrived at the tree? Partaking of the fruit of the tree—the love of God.

In our day, a prophet, Ezra Taft Benson, taught the same truth:

"Why did God put the first commandment first? Because He knew that if we truly loved Him we would want to keep all of His other commandments. . . .

"We must put God in the forefront of everything else in our lives. . . .

"When we put God first, all other things fall into their proper place or drop out of our lives. Our love of the Lord will govern the claims for our affection, the demands on our time, the interests we pursue, and the order of our priorities.

"We should put God ahead of *everyone else* in our lives" ("The Great Commandment—Love the Lord," 4).

SCRIPTURAL ILLUSTRATIONS

Examples permeate scripture showing blessings and opportunities available to those who put God first in their lives. Scripture equally testifies to the misery and woe that follow those who put anyone or anything else as a higher priority than the Lord. Remember Cain, who once hearkened to the voice of the Lord as well as to his brother Abel? (Moses 5:26). The details are not given, but Cain submerged God in his priority list. In verse 18, we read, "And Cain loved Satan more than God." At that point, Cain would probably still claim he loved God, just not as much as Satan. After that priority flip-flop, his declaration, "Who is the Lord that I should know him?" is not a major leap (Moses 5:16). Neither is his subsequent disdain for Abel, his alienation from his parents, and finally his being shut out from God's presence.

But the adversary is not always so blatant. He doesn't often insist that we put *him* first in our loyalty. Anything or anyone other than God as the primary object of our love will suffice. Such subtlety is apparent in a national Gallup survey that considered beliefs of college-educated Christians in comparison to responses of those without college education on several religious topics. The results showed that "college graduates are about three times more likely than persons without college education to put the Second Commandment (loving your neighbor) ahead of the First Commandment (loving God)." Notice what naturally follows those who take God out of first place, according to the same survey. "The better educated are also about three times as likely to think it possible to be a true Christian without believing in the divinity of Christ" (Wuthnow, *Restructuring of American Religion*, 169).

All too frequently in today's world, a Christian is defined

on the basis of the horizontal relationship between oneself and "neighbor" rather than the vertical relationship with Deity. In this distorted view of Christianity, our relationship with others becomes more important than loving God, having faith in Christ, and being a devoted disciple of His gospel. If God isn't first, sooner or later He will simply be a nice embellishment to our lives. When we put God first, we are empowered to love each other better, even if our love is not at first understood. The trouble is that too often we ignore things that should be first in our lives and go after secondary things, thereby losing both. As C. S. Lewis observed, "You can get second things only by putting first things first" ("First and Second Things," in *God in the Dock,* 280).

Consider an extreme case involving the Nephite army during Mormon's life. They chose to turn away from God, concluding their strength and savvy alone were sufficient to defeat the Lamanites and retain their lands. These godless Nephites identified their purpose for fighting. Notice not only who is listed first in their cause but who doesn't even make the list: "They would stand boldly before the Lamanites and fight for their wives, and their children, and their houses, and their homes" (Mormon 2:23).

While the language is reminiscent of the Title of Liberty— clearly Captain Moroni also included wives and children in their great cause—Moroni put God first. "In memory of our God," Moroni wrote on the torn piece of his coat, "our religion, and freedom, and our peace, our wives, and our children" (Alma 46:12). Captain Moroni's army remembered to pray and to heed the direction of righteous leaders, and they were victorious in miraculous ways. God actually fought their battles for them and preserved their freedom, families, and homes. By contrast, the army during Mormon's time lost everything. Their families in particular suffered. Mormon noted the awful results: "O the depravity of my people! . . . they delight in everything save that which is good; and the suffering of our women and our children upon all the face of this land doth exceed everything" (Moroni 9:18–19). Here was a people who went after secondary things, setting God aside, and lost everything.

Another example shows blessings for a family when the mother puts God first. The Lord promised Abraham that His gospel would go first to the children of Abraham and from them to the rest of the world. Jesus encountered a Gentile woman from Syro-Phoenicia who pressed Him to make an exception to that promise. She knew who Jesus was: "Have mercy on me, O Lord, thou son of David." She had a plea, not for herself, but for a beloved family member: "My daughter is grievously vexed with a devil." Her reaction to the Savior's response indicates the order of her priorities. First the Savior ignored her by "answer[ing] her not a word," and "his disciples came and besought him, saying, Send her away; for she crieth after us." Jesus explained to her, "I am not sent but unto the lost sheep of the house of Israel," finally telling her, "It is not meet to take the children's bread, and to cast it to dogs." He just called her a dog! (Matthew 15:22–24, 26).

If we were in her place, and we loved family more than God, how would we respond to the Savior's apparent rebuff? We would most likely be offended and furiously depart, concluding that *we* could find a solution for our family without Him. In consequence, what would happen to our loved one? What would happen to us?

But that is not the way this Gentile woman reacted. She refused to be offended. On the contrary, she continued to worship the Savior, communicating that she didn't expect the full feast, only a few crumbs such as those that fall from the table. The consequence? Her daughter was healed, and the woman was blessed for her remarkable faith in Christ. Such a positive outcome does not imply an absence of hard times in the future. After her interaction with this Jewish holy man, her own people likely persecuted her. But she had discovered the power of faith in Christ, which would strengthen her in the face of any hardship.

Scribes and Pharisees who calculated tithing to the mint leaf were offended because Jesus did not require hand washing before eating. They, who loved the praise of men more than the praise of God, lost all. This Syro-Phoenician woman, by putting her love for the Lord first, gained more than she had ever imagined.

INSPIRATION FROM LOVING GOD

The answer to frustrations about what we should be doing—today, next week, and next year—lies in where God figures in our lives. By changing our focus from seeking praise from our peers to finding acceptance in God, our capacity and wisdom increase, enabling us to progressively follow all that God commands. Such nagging thoughts as "I don't think I can ever make it" or "Have I done enough?" will be replaced with greater love for God and losing ourselves in His service.

"Now, my dear sisters," President Gordon B. Hinckley counseled, "you are doing the best you can, and that best results in good to yourself and to others. Do not nag yourself with a sense of failure. Get on your knees and ask for the blessings of the Lord; then stand on your feet and do what you are asked to do. Then leave the matter in the hands of the Lord. You will discover that you have accomplished something beyond price" ("To the Women of the Church," 114).

The Apostle Paul testified, "I can do all things through Christ which strengtheneth me" (Philippians 4:13). In similar language, after his fourteen-year mission among the Lamanites, Ammon rejoiced, "I know that I am nothing; as to my strength I am weak; therefore I will not boast of myself, but I will boast of my God, for in his strength I can do all things" (Alma 26:12).

At the Last Supper, Jesus taught the Apostles: "A new commandment I give unto you, That ye love one another; as I have loved you, that ye also love one another. By this shall all men know that ye are my disciples, if ye have love one to another" (John 13:34–35).

How is this commandment new? How does it differ from the first two great commandments, to love God with all our heart and to love our neighbor as ourselves? When Christ's love is our example, we rejoice in our neighbor's success and appreciate each person's unique contribution without denigrating ourselves. We don't lose hope for improvement when our own best efforts seem inadequate.

When this highest love of God comes before any checklist obedience, humility and gratitude accompany our sincere efforts, and we are empowered beyond our natural ability to "go and do" what the Lord commands (1 Nephi 3:7).

Furthermore, when we are filled with God's love, His

commandments cease to be a burden because they actually inspire us (D&C 20:7). From this new perspective, we discover the principle behind the cautions and commands and experience a new level of joy in obedience. Frequent opportunities to become "witnesses of God at all times and in all things, and in all places" unfold naturally in our daily lives (Mosiah 18:9). Our prayers project a powerful communication with God instead of vain repetitions. Our relationships with others become more genuine and satisfying. Education produces greater meaning and even a sense of divine purpose. Our scripture study forgets measuring pages or minutes as our hearts and minds are illuminated by the sweet doctrine of the gospel. As President Howard W. Hunter profoundly taught, "If our lives and our faith are centered on Jesus Christ and his restored gospel, nothing can ever go permanently wrong. On the other hand, if our lives are not centered on the Savior and his teachings, no other success can ever be permanently right" (*Teachings of Howard W. Hunter*, 40).

WHAT COMES SECOND

Setting priorities is not a problem of time; we each have exactly the same amount allotted each day. With increasing opportunities to learn and to serve and so many good causes that would benefit from our help, we will always have more on our daily list than we can accomplish. That is where Martha and Mary help us to remember. We may not accomplish number ten or even number three on our daily list, but we will most assuredly get to number one.

When God comes first in our lives, whatever comes second will likely change tomorrow. Furthermore, whatever comes second for me will likely be different for you. When God comes first in our lives, however, whatever comes second will always be right. Like Mary, Hugh Nibley found that gospel study is especially powerful as a means to know what should come second on any given day. He observed that if you're not sure what you should be doing, read particularly the Book of Mormon. It is either the best thing you could be doing at the time or it will quickly put you on to what you should be doing (*Teachings of the Book of Mormon,* 2).

Putting God first supplies direction to our quest for balance, for finding the One Needful Thing whose gifts cannot be taken from us. Seeing Mary and Martha contentedly engaged in serving the Lord, using talents and spiritual direction they were gifted to offer, is yet another marvelous example of the miracle. All are blessed when their hearts are turned to the Lord. All are blessed with reverence for Jesus Christ because they desired to put Him first. Rather than compare and rank their different modes of service, they loved God first.

Without seeking attention from others, they put the focus on the Lord. Such consecrated service invited the witness of the Spirit to guide others to Christ. As the sisters of Bethany embrace that which cannot be taken from them, Mary and Martha likewise invite each of us to come unto Christ.

CHAPTER EIGHT

Wait Upon the Lord

Various New Testament manuscripts give slightly different wording for the phrase the King James Bible translates "one thing is needful" (Luke 10:41). Of particular note is the John Wycliffe Bible, widely accepted as the first English translation. Wycliffe, translating from Latin, interpreted the phrase to communicate an even greater sense of privation: "one thing is necessary." When we find the One who is necessary, even essential, we receive that which shall not be taken from us.

From assorted challenges, diverse gifts, unique personalities, and varied contributions, Mary and Martha lead us to the Necessary One—Jesus Christ. Like the sisters of Bethany, we do not fully acknowledge Him as necessary until we confront our lost and fallen condition without Him. Most often that occurs when we face a crisis greater than alternative methods can help us to survive. In such dire circumstances, when neither our finest skills nor those of anyone else on earth are effective, we become profoundly humble. We cry out to the One who is necessary, and we wait—wait for Him—because we realize that no other power can rescue us.

OUR REQUIREMENT TO WAIT

If we will let Him, God will take us to that place where no one can help us but Him. Arriving at that place will always require us to wait upon the Lord. I have wondered if this is the place where Grandma had come that inspired our gospel discussions. In such circumstances we most deeply appreciate Nephi's stirring declaration, "For we know it is by grace that we are saved, after all we can do" (2 Nephi 25:23).

The concept of waiting seems counterintuitive in a frantic, chaotic world. Nothing less than instant gratification is acceptable in such a society. We want results today, eliminating all consternation from the unknown. Perhaps that is one reason why scripture reinforces that our responsibility in salvation depends not upon our merits but on our faith in Christ. And faith in Christ requires us to wait for Him. Inspired by Isaiah's testimony and his own life's experiences, the Book of Mormon prophet Jacob taught: "And the people of the Lord shall not be ashamed. For the people of the Lord are they who wait for him; for they still wait for the coming of the Messiah" (2 Nephi 6:13; see also 1 Nephi 21:23; Isaiah 49:23).

Jesus communicated the need to wait in teaching preparation for His Second Coming. His message was not one of sitting idly, without responsibility and effort, but of actively looking forward with confident patience and expectation: "Let your loins be girded about, and your lights burning; and ye yourselves like unto [those] that wait for their lord. . . . Blessed are those servants, whom the lord when he cometh shall find watching. . . . Be ye therefore ready also: for the Son of man cometh at an hour when ye think not" (Luke 12:35–40).

For those who faithfully wait, the Lord promised compensatory blessings to enable success and fulfillment: "They that wait upon the Lord shall renew their strength; they shall mount up with wings as eagles; they shall run, and not be weary; and they shall walk, and not faint" (Isaiah 40:31). Mary and Martha experienced that requisite waiting and the Lord's abundant response when their brother Lazarus fell seriously ill and died.

MARTHA'S TESTIMONY OF THE RESURRECTION

The operative word in the miracle of Christ raising Lazarus from the dead is *wait.* The scriptural narrative thereby reminds us that God's blessings when we choose that part which shall not be taken occur according to His timetable, not ours. After hearing that Lazarus was sick in Bethany, Jesus *waited* two more days in Perea before commencing His trek back to Judea. Mary and Martha sent word to Jesus that His friend and their brother was sick, but they were required to *wait* several days for a response. Jesus explained to His disciples that Lazarus's "sickness is not unto death, but for the glory of God" and "to the intent [they] may believe" (John 11:4, 15). Learning that Lazarus did in reality die, these believers were required to *wait* to finally understand what Jesus meant. He orchestrated this moment for much more than merely allaying fears and preventing pain. He is the Redeemer as well as the Master Teacher. Jesus purposefully delayed His arrival in Bethany to help His disciples understand the transcendent truth of resurrection, made clearer precisely by the necessity to wait.

When Jesus met Martha on the outskirts of Bethany, He told her, "Thy brother shall rise again" (Luke 11:23). Martha's calm response to the Savior, after this unexplained requirement to wait, would surprise us if we had not noted her changed heart since the previous October. Mary and Martha had put all their trust and faith in Christ. As soon as Lazarus fell seriously ill, they sent for Him as the only hope to save their brother. They had perfect faith that if Jesus came, He would cure Lazarus. But Jesus delayed His coming—until Lazarus died. What response would be more typical in this setting? Disappointment? Frustration? Anger? More easily, we might expect Martha to echo her earlier complaint, "Lord, don't you care?" We could imagine her pouting accusation, "I thought we were your friends. You must love others more than you love us. Why did you make us wait?" None of these complaints, however, color Martha's reaction. She communicated neither bitterness nor accusations against Jesus. Like Mary, she had found the One Necessary, and her entire hope resided in Him. By delaying His return, Jesus led Mary and Martha to the edge of their faith. That is the place where He can teach us most of all.

Without understanding His purpose in waiting, Martha's response reflected her stretched faith, "I know that he shall rise again in the resurrection at the last day" (John 11:24). The Savior testified to Martha:

"I am the resurrection, and the life: he that believeth in me, though he were dead, yet shall he live:

"And whosoever liveth and believeth in me shall never die. Believest thou this?

"She saith unto him, Yea, Lord: I believe that thou art the Christ, the Son of God, which should come into the world" (John 11:24–27).

Before Christ's example as the firstfruits of the literal resurrection, Martha's faith and testimony in the Savior are noteworthy. Her witness echoes that of the Apostle Peter (Matthew 16:13–16). Elder Bruce R. McConkie observed: "Women as well as men have testimonies, receive revelation from the Spirit, and know of themselves of the Lord's divinity. Martha's testimony of Christ's divine Sonship is as plain, positive, and sure as was the same testimony borne by Peter" (*Doctrinal New Testament Commentary*, 1:532). By a requirement to wait upon the Lord, Martha and Mary were profoundly strengthened to surmount an even greater loss with the Savior's departure.

In contemplation of their maturing faith and application of Christ's teachings since they first hosted Him, we are likewise invited to trust the Lord in our times of trial. Sister Patricia T. Holland accepted their invitation with these results:

"On a pristinely clear and beautifully bright day, I sat overlooking the sea of Galilee and reread Luke 10:38. But instead of the words there on the page, I thought I saw with my mind and heard with my heart these words: 'Pat, Pat, thou art careful and troubled about many things.' Then the power of pure and personal revelation seized me as I read, 'But one thing [only one thing] is truly needful . . .'

"Spirit to spirit, our loving Father in Heaven seemed to be

whispering to me, 'You don't have to worry over so many things. The one thing that is needful—the only thing that is truly needful—is to keep your eyes toward . . . my Son.' 'Learn of me,' he seemed to say, 'and listen to my words; walk in the meekness of my Spirit, and you shall have peace in me' (D&C 19:23). Suddenly I did have peace. I knew . . . that my life had always been in his hands—from the very beginning! And so are the lives of all of you, of every woman who wants to do right and grows in capacity and tries to give all she can" ("Many Things . . . One Thing," 190–91).

Even in our purely Martha-esque moments, when we show our testimonies more by our active works than by our words, we see the Lord's requirement to wait. In those moments when all our faculties are tuned to Him, our strength is renewed, our focus sharpened, and we are enabled to work miracles in His name.

THE WOMAN OF PROVERBS 31

So what of the Proverbs 31 woman, whose price is above rubies? How do Mary's and Martha's lessons apply to the perfectionist-sounding characteristics derived from her example? As a young college student, I wanted to become like her and do everything perfectly well. To speed up the process,

I made a list of her attributes so that I could focus on one every month until I had conquered them all.

The older I became, however, the more I hated the list. Sewing for family (v. 13), cooking exotic meals (v. 14), getting up before sunrise to prepare a fine breakfast (v. 15), growing a garden (v. 16), even having strong arms, which I interpreted as being not flabby and so required lifting weights (v. 17). The list continued. The verse that describes this ideal woman's attitude through all this perfect service, "in her tongue is the law of kindness" (v. 26), was the final straw. I had to work and serve my family day and night and stay cheerful all the while! It was impossible, I concluded, and the reason Mother's Day programs in the Church are so often the worst day of the year for mothers. And I didn't even have children!

In a knee-jerk reaction, I found ways to make fun of the Proverbs passage to avoid taking it seriously. Her price is above rubies. But what about diamonds? Or a new sports car? Is she worth that much? "She is like the merchants' ships; she bringeth her food from afar" (v. 14) became for me: "Put all the kids in the minivan; we're going for take-out."

My adverse reactions to the Proverbs 31 passage ignored what Mary and Martha learned. My approach overlooked the One who is necessary. My blindness occurred because I sought solutions without putting God first.

I have since learned to look for Christ in a scriptural passage when my understanding is blocked. Where is Jesus Christ in Proverbs 31? I found Him in verse 25: "Strength and honour are her clothing." A Hebrew word used in Old Testament references for Christ's merciful Atonement is *kaphar*. For example, *kaphar* is in the holy day, Yom Kippur (Day of Atonement) and the mercy seat (seat of *kaphar*) in the Holy of Holies. *Kaphar* means "to cover" or "a covering." Applied to the Atonement of Christ, it communicates obliteration of sin, protection, and covering of debt. Once the word's general meaning is understood, the imagery of Christ's all-powerful covering can be seen everywhere in scripture, even when the specific word *kaphar* does not appear. In the case of Proverbs 31, for example, imagery of Christ and His Atonement is recognizable as a covering symbolized by the woman's "clothing."

"Strength and honour are her clothing," the passage teaches. In other words, Christ is the woman's source of strength and her honor. What then makes her arms strong to accomplish all that the day requires? The Savior's enabling power. The snow that she does not fear in verse 21 could symbolically be sin, or trials, or the need to wait. She doesn't fear the snow because she clothes her household in scarlet, another symbol of Christ's sacrifice. Otherwise stated, she leads her family to Christ, who covers them in a way that she never could. He covers her family with that which shall not be taken from them. On resurrection morning, her children will assuredly rise up and call the Savior blessed because of His mercy, merits, and grace that make resurrection an unconditional gift for them. Proverbs 31 also teaches that "her children arise up, and call her blessed" (v. 28). Because of her role in providing them physical bodies and leading them to their Redeemer, her children will also arise at the resurrection to call their mother "blessed."

Interestingly, the same Hebrew word rendered "virtuous" to characterize this Proverbs 31 woman is translated "strong," "mighty," or "powerful" to describe an army, King David in battle, or the power of horses (Psalm 33:17; 2 Samuel 22:40). In other words, Proverbs 31:10 could just as easily read, "Who can find a strong, mighty, and powerful woman?" She it is who "feareth the Lord" (v. 30), who has found the only One who is essential.

In a world where multitasking is an art and appetites are never satiated, we try to get our heads and hearts around "one thing is needful" (Luke 10:42). Like Mary and Martha, only when we turn our lives over to the Savior do we receive that which cannot be taken from us. With our hearts and heads riveted on Him, the Savior's grace makes us equal to whatever He commands. With His enabling power, we receive the peace of the Spirit and strength beyond our natural abilities to do and be whatever He asks.

Grandma's Lesson through a Quilt

Without question, Grandma Harris helped me better understand and appreciate Martha. And Martha helped me better appreciate and understand Grandma. In an attempt to be true to Grandma when I began writing this book, I decided to make a quilt—for the first time in my life. Our daughter wanted to replace an aging, beloved quilt she used as a bed-spread. It was a solid-colored piece of fabric, quilted from a pattern, just like quilts Grandma used to make. I asked if I could make a replacement quilt. She offered me a remarkable gift by saying yes.

My mother helped me select one of Grandma's numerous quilt patterns that she had inherited. When she saw my enthusiasm, Mom also bequeathed me Grandma's little golden thimble. I borrowed quilting frames and quilt-marking skills from a friend and finally was ready to begin.

The day I put the quilt on the frames was magical. As I prepared to make the first stitch, I couldn't help but stop and savor the experience. The stretched fabric taking up much of the room seemed to beckon Grandma to pull up a chair across from me and pick up a threaded needle. I suddenly had an overwhelming feeling that she was keenly aware of me in that moment—and immensely proud of my courage to follow her example. She seemed to be telling me that she appreciated what I had taught her but that she had also learned some things she wanted to teach me.

Amazingly, I finished the quilt long before I finished writing the book. Returning to the soon-familiar pattern was a welcome reward after long days of work at the university. Somewhere between the thousands of repetitious stitches, up and down, and up and down, I found a pleasant way to be still and savor the wonder of God's grace granted during the day. Did Grandma find the same solace around her quilts? Was that where she pondered and received His strength to pursue all the demands of her days? As a type of Christ's enabling power, a quilt is, after all, a covering, a covering that communicates love in every stitch. And like the Proverbs 31 woman, "she maketh herself coverings of tapestry" that give her "strength and honour" (vv. 22, 25).

MUTUAL INFLUENCE

Whenever I now go to Relief Society and observe the familiar paintings of Mary and Martha hosting Jesus in Bethany, I see reflections of their mature faith in Christ. I perceive their

Jesus at the Home of Mary and Martha, by Minerva Teichert

abiding love for the Lord, their mutual appreciation, and evidence of their subsequent influence on each other.

In all the paintings, Mary is still at the feet of the Savior but now seems genuinely appreciative of Martha's feast. Martha is still doing something—mixing something in a bowl (in the Del Parson painting) or serving an enormous Thanksgiving turkey (in the Minerva Teichert work)—but she is also keenly listening to the Lord. I like to think that Martha learns more by doing something while listening rather than being forced to sit still all the time. Mary and Martha have both chosen "that good part" (Luke 10:42)—that is, they put Christ first in their lives while being true to their God-given gifts.

None of us is either a Martha or a Mary. Fortunately, mutually exclusive categories delineated by a few verses in scripture do not define any of us. We are each a marvelous, unique creation of God, seasoned by interaction with other remarkable people, including those in scripture. Like Mary and Martha, we need one another and are blessed by our associations, but our purpose is not to become a replica of Mary, Martha, or the "ideal" member of our ward.

ONE THING IS NEEDFUL

Our purpose is to become like Jesus Christ—the only One who is necessary. He is the Anchor to stabilize our wandering souls and the only Example that never disappoints. Through His infinite covering, which "is broad as eternity" (Moses 7:53), and our faith in Him, He empowers each of us to be "sure and steadfast, always abounding in good works" (Ether 12:4), and we freely give Him the glory.

Mary and Martha's secret to a harmonious, fulfilling life is neither discovering more time, nor transforming themselves to be like the other, nor gaining notoriety for their remarkable gifts. More important than specific talents in the home or the office or the ability to remember and recite scripture, Mary and Martha found the One Needful Thing that would not be taken from them.

They wholeheartedly came to the Essential One and were consequently covered by His enabling power. His grace is sufficient. Sufficient means enough. His wisdom and strength are enough to cover us, to see us through all our chaotic todays and turbulent tomorrows. Mary and Martha's witness, borne more powerfully than words through their example of discipleship, echo Moroni's invitation to each of us:

"Yea, come unto Christ, and *be perfected in him,* and deny yourselves of all ungodliness; and if ye shall deny yourselves of all ungodliness, and love God with all your might, mind and strength, then is *his grace sufficient for you,* that *by His grace ye may be perfect in Christ;* and if by the grace of God ye are

perfect in Christ, ye can in nowise deny the power of God"
(Moroni 10:32; emphasis added).

This is the good news of the gospel of Christ. This is what
shall not be taken from us. Praise be to the sisters of Bethany
for leading us to the One.

Sources

Allen-Pratt, Kelli. "Confessions of a Perfectionist." *Ensign,* June 2005, 65.

Asay, Carlos E. "Rooted and Built Up in Christ." In *The Old Testament and the Latter-day Saints.* Sidney B. Sperry Symposium series. Salt Lake City: Randall Book, 1986.

Ashton, Marvin J. "The Tongue Can Be a Sharp Sword." *Ensign,* May 1992, 18.

Benson, Ezra Taft. "The Great Commandment—Love the Lord." *Ensign,* May 1988, 4.

Brown, C. Louise. "Walking in the World: An Immersion in Service." Address to a conference at Brigham Young University, "Approaching a School of Zion," Provo, Utah, March 1993.

Brown, Raymond E. *The Gospel According to John.* 2 vols. Anchor Bible Series, vols. 29 and 29A. Garden City, N.Y.: Doubleday, 1966–70.

Carmack, John K. "Lord, Increase Our Faith." *Ensign,* March 2002, 56.

Drummond, Henry. *The Greatest Thing in the World.* New York: Dodge, n.d.

Farrar, Frederic W. *The Life of Christ.* New York: Doubleday, 1898. Reprint, Salt Lake City: Bookcraft, 1994.

Forbes, B. C. In *Reader's Digest,* October 1983, cover.

Gillieson, T. "A Plea for Proportion: St. Luke x.38–42." *Expository Times* 59 (1947–48): 111.

Harvey, Shirley Adwena. "To Mary—Who Sat at Jesus' Feet." *Ensign,* December 1982, 49.

Hinckley, Gordon B. "Resolve to Keep Balance in Your Lives." Address delivered at Logan, Utah, 21 October 1997. *Church News,* 1 November 1997.

———. "To the Women of the Church." *Ensign,* November 2003, 113.

Holland, Patricia Terry. "Many Things . . . One Thing." *The Best of Women's Conference.* Salt Lake City: Bookcraft, 2000.

Hunter, Howard W. *The Teachings of Howard W. Hunter.* Edited by Clyde J. Williams. Salt Lake City, Utah: Deseret Book, 2002.

Hymns of The Church of Jesus Christ of Latter-day Saints. Salt Lake City: The Church of Jesus Christ of Latter-day Saints, 1985.

Kimball, Spencer W. "In Love and Power and without Fear." *New Era,* July 1981, 8.

———. *The Teachings of Spencer W. Kimball.* Edited by Edward L. Kimball. Salt Lake City, Utah: Bookcraft, 1982.

Lewis, C. S. *God in the Dock: Essays on Theology and Ethics.* Edited by Walter Hooper. Grand Rapids, Mich.: Eerdmans, 1970.

Matthews, Victor H. *Manners and Customs in the Bible.* Rev. ed. Peabody, Mass.: Hendrickson Publishers, 1991.

McConkie, Bruce R. *Doctrinal New Testament Commentary.* 3 vols. Salt Lake City: Deseret Book, 1965–73.

McCullough, David. *1776.* New York: Simon and Schuster, 2005.

Nibley, Hugh. *Teachings of the Book of Mormon, Semester 1.* Provo,

Utah: Foundation for Ancient Research and Mormon Studies, 1993.

Oaks, Dallin H. *Pure in Heart.* Salt Lake City: Bookcraft, 1988.

O'Rahilly, A. "The Two Sisters." *Scripture* 4 (1949–51): 69.

Parry, Catherine Corman. "Simon, I Have Somewhat to Say unto Thee: Judgment and Condemnation in the Parables of Jesus." In *Brigham Young University 1990–1991 Devotional and Fireside Speeches.* Provo, Utah: Brigham Young University, 1991.

Reid, Barbara E. *Choosing the Better Part? Women in the Gospel of Luke.* Collegeville, Minn.: The Liturgical Press, 1996.

Scott, Richard G. "First Things First." *Ensign,* May 2001, 7.

Smith, Joseph F., Anthon H. Lund, and Charles W. Penrose. "A Warning Voice." *Improvement Era,* September 1913, 1148.

Talmage, James E. *Jesus the Christ.* 3d ed. Salt Lake City: The Church of Jesus Christ of Latter-day Saints, 1916.

———. "The Parable of the Grateful Cat." *Improvement Era,* August 1916, 877–78.

Wirthlin, Joseph B. "The Virtue of Kindness." *Ensign,* May 2005, 28.

Wuthnow, Robert. *The Restructuring of American Religion.* Princeton, N.J.: Princeton University Press, 1988.

Index

setting, 97–98; scriptural
illustrations of, 98–103; God
as first, 103–5; second,
105–7
Prodigal son, parable of, 65–66

Quilt, 119–20

Receiving, 36, 93
Reed, Joseph, 62–64
Relief Society, 2, 3
Repentance, 62
Resurrection, 25–26, 111–15
Rituals, 34

Sacrifice, 40, 42, 83
Samaritan, good, 19, 46, 93
Satan, 46, 96, 99
Sayings, 31
Scott, Richard G., 96
Scriptures: women in, 3–8,
115–19; pondering, 10; com-
muning with God through,
13–14; applying, 28; women's
knowledge of, 72
Second Coming, 111
Selflessness, 48, 93
Self-righteousness, 44
Self-worth, 45
Servant, 22, 39–40, 35–38
Service: grandmother offered,

2–3, 11; comparison of, 13,
23, 66–67; cumbered, 33, 35,
38–39, 43, 45, 48; Christ
offered, 36–38; receiving, 36,
93; with no thought of
reward, 40, 49, 86; to God,
42; motivation for, 46–49;
judgmental, 60; condemning
another's, 51–67; through listening and learning, 71–74;
delight in, 85; secret, 85–89;
and anonymity, 89–91
Simon, 26–28
Sins, 65
Smith, Joseph, 43
Spikenard, 77
Spirit, 11, 13
Success, 12, 44, 86

Talents, 54, 66
Talmage, James E., 40–42, 78
Teichert, Minerva, 121
Television, 73
Temper, 65–66
Temple, 20
"To Mary—Who Sat at Jesus'
Feet," 70
Troubled, 34

Unprofitable servant, parable of,
22, 39–40